Sew It for Christmas™

Edited by Barbara Weiland

HOUSE of
WHITE
BIRCHES

PUBLISHERS
SINCE 1947

Sew It For Christmas

EDITOR	Barbara Weiland
ART DIRECTOR	Brad Snow
PUBLISHING SERVICES DIRECTOR	Brenda Gallmeyer
MANAGING EDITOR	Sue Reeves
ASSISTANT ART DIRECTOR	Nick Pierce
COPY SUPERVISOR	Michelle Beck
COPY EDITORS	Nicki Lehman, Mary O'Donnell, Judy Weatherford
GRAPHIC ARTS SUPERVISOR	Ronda Bechinski
BOOK DESIGN	Amy S. Lin
GRAPHIC ARTISTS	Glenda Chamberlain, Edith Teegarden
PRODUCTION ASSISTANTS	Marj Morgan, Judy Neuenschwander
TECHNICAL ARTIST	Nicole Gage
PHOTOGRAPHY SUPERVISOR	Tammy Christian
PHOTOGRAPHY	Don Clark, Matthew Owen, Jackie Schaffel
PHOTO STYLISTS	Tammy Steiner, Tammy M. Smith
CHIEF EXECUTIVE OFFICER	David J. McKee
BOOK MARKETING DIRECTOR	Dwight Seward

Printed in China
First Printing: 2007
Library of Congress Control Number: 2006932194
Hardcover ISBN: 978-1-59217-166-8
Softcover ISBN: 978-1-59217-167-5

DRGbooks.com

1 2 3 4 5 6 7 8 9

Contents

Christmas Just for Fun!

Poinsettia Warmers 6

Christmas Carryall 10

Christmas Countdown 15

Pinwheel Candies 20

Jingle Bell Cards 26

Sock-It-to-Me Knit Wits 30

Pet Hang-Ups 36

Mitten Gift Bags 40

Deck the Halls

Hanky-Panky Stockings 46

On, Dancer! 51

Homespun Christmas 58

Christmas Sew-Phisticates 66

The Gifted Mantel 74

'Tis the Season 78

Angelina Poinsettias 86

Partridge on a Pillow 94

The Birds' Christmas 98

Christmas Framed 102

Snowmen on Ice 106

Set the Holiday Table

Holiday Reverses 112

Crazy for Christmas 118

Star Bright Place Setting 124

Pieced Elegance 131

Oh, Tannenbaum! 134

Dress for the Season

Winter in Bloom 140

Tree-Time Top 145

Strippy Christmas Style 152

Wrapped in Ruffles 157

Holiday Cardigans 164

Pretty Packages 170

Fabric & Supplies, **175**   Sewing Sources, **175**   Special Thanks, **176**

Merry Christmas!

It may not be Christmas when you open the pages of this book, but to my mind, it can be Christmas at my sewing machine all year long. It's never too early or too late to start on my Christmas sewing list. You may feel the same way. Christmas sewing is just as much fun in April, July and October, or any month for that matter, as it is in November and December!

In the pages that follow, you'll find plenty of holiday-themed projects to inspire your sewing now and for the months to come. Choose from a range of fun garments, from fine and fancy to homespun. Wrap up in a pretty ruffled shawl, or cozy up in a homespun cardigan fashioned from a simple sweatshirt—a great gift to sew in a hurry. Check out the Dress for the Season section for more wonderful wearables.

If Christmas decorating is on your list, the wonderful selection of decorating projects in Deck the Halls and Set the Holiday Table await your stitching pleasure—colorful pillows, table runners, place mats and napkins, not to mention beautiful mantel covers, stockings, ornaments and tree skirts. You're sure to love Oh, Tannenbaum! on page 134—the almost-no-sew Christmas trees for holiday decorating. Make trees for yourself or to give as gifts, or sell at your Christmas bazaar and use up lots of fabric leftovers and embellishments from your stash. There's a fun snowman quilt to sew, too. And Christmas

Just for Fun!, beginning on page 5, offers projects with a touch of whimsy or warmth that will tickle you or someone you know.

Have fun making your list and checking it twice as you peruse the projects and choose those you just must sew now!

Warm regards,

Christmas Just for Fun!

It's the season for sewing fun. In the pages to come you'll find projects to brighten your holiday home and heart. Stitch up a cozy throw and matching pillow. Make a giant carryall to tote your gifts to Grandma's house, or cut and sew a special Advent calendar for the kids to count down the days til Santa's arrival. There are stockings for your pets and more fun projects ahead to stitch up some lighthearted Christmas cheer.

Poinsettia Warmers

Designs by Lorine Mason

Deep scarlet poinsettia leaves contrast beautifully against ivory fleece in this warming duo. Share your Christmas spirit by creating this warm throw and 3-D pillow to give as gifts or to add a spot of holiday color and warmth to your family room.

Finished Sizes
Pillow: 18 inches square
Throw: 40 x 46 inches

Materials
• 54-inch-wide polyester fleece
    1¾ yards ivory
    ½ yard scarlet
• Scrap gold fleece
• 2 (⅞-inch-diameter) buttons
• 12-inch-square ready-made pillow form
• All-purpose thread to match fabrics
• Water-soluble marking pen
• Long hand-sewing or doll needle
• Permanent fabric adhesive
• Safety pin
• White paper and pencil
• Basic sewing tools and equipment

Cutting
• From the ivory fleece, cut two 18-inch squares. Place squares wrong sides together with raw edges even and round off the corners by drawing around the edge of a small plate to mark the cutting lines. Cut along the marked lines through both layers at each corner (Figure 1).

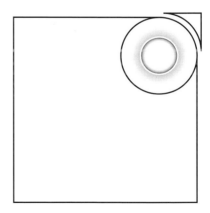

Figure 1
Use a small plate as a guide for rounding the corners.

• From the remaining ivory fleece, cut one 40 x 46-inch rectangle for the throw and one 1½ x 14-inch strip for the bow. Round off the corners of the throw as shown for the pillow.

- Enlarge the poinsettia patterns on page 9 as directed onto paper. For the pillow, trace seven large leaves, five medium leaves and five small leaves on white paper. Cut out each shape with at least a ½-inch-wide margin beyond the drawn lines.
- Fold the scarlet felt in half with wrong sides facing and pin the leaf patterns in place. Stitch through the paper pattern ⅛ inch inside the drawn outer line. Tear away the paper pattern and stitch the leaf veins referring to the patterns for placement. Cut out each leaf ⅛ inch from the outer stitching.
- For the throw, cut three medium and two small scarlet leaves (single-layer).
- From the gold fleece, cut eight ¾ x 2-inch strips for the poinsettia center.

Pillow Assembly

1. Select a decorative stitch on your machine and stitch ½ inch from the outer edges of one pillow square. Trim close to the outer edge of the stitching, taking care not to clip the stitches. Repeat on the pillow back.

2. On the pillow front only, add two more rows of decorative stitching spaced 1 inch apart.

3. Use the water-soluble marking pen to draw a 12-inch square in the center of the pillow top on the right side. Mark the center point on the right side of the pillow front and the pillow back. With wrong sides facing, pin the pillow front to the pillow back. Stitch through both layers along the drawn line leaving a 4-inch-long section unstitched (Figure 2).

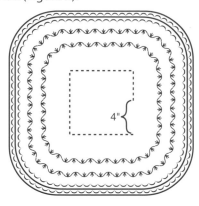

Figure 2
Stitch layers together on drawn line, leaving 4"-long opening.

4. Insert the pillow form and complete the stitching.

5. Mark the center point on the pillow front and back. Using a long hand-sewing needle with doubled, waxed thread, take a stitch on the pillow top to anchor the threads. Bring the needle and thread up through one hole in the button and down through the next, and then through the pillow cover and pillow form to the back. Add the other button and stitch back through the layers to the top button. As you sew, pull the threads taut to create a "dimple" in the center of the pillow. Tie off the threads securely to anchor the stitching.

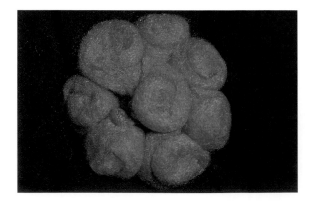

6. Center the seven largest poinsettia leaves on the pillow front, overlapping them and covering the center button. Using a needle and thread, stitch the bottom leaves to the pillow top along the lower edge of each leaf. Arrange the five medium leaves on top of the large ones and stitch in place. Add the five small leaves in the same manner.

7. Tightly roll each gold fleece strip. Center the rolls on the poinsettia and glue in place. Place a heavy object on top and allow to dry thoroughly.

Throw Assembly

1. Select a decorative stitch on your machine and stitch ½ inch from the outer edges of the throw. Trim close to the stitching. Add two more rows of decorative stitching spaced 1 inch apart.

Note: *Since you are stitching around a large square, it's essential to check your bobbin thread supply often so you won't run out in the middle of a row of stitching.*

2. Arrange three medium leaves at one corner of the throw; stitch in place ¼ inch from the outer edges of each one. Stitch the veins.

3. Add two small leaves and stitch in place; add veins.

4. Fold the ivory fleece strip in half lengthwise and stitch ⅜ inch from the raw edges. Turn the tube right side out and tie into a bow. Position at the upper end of the leaves and sew in place securely. ✦

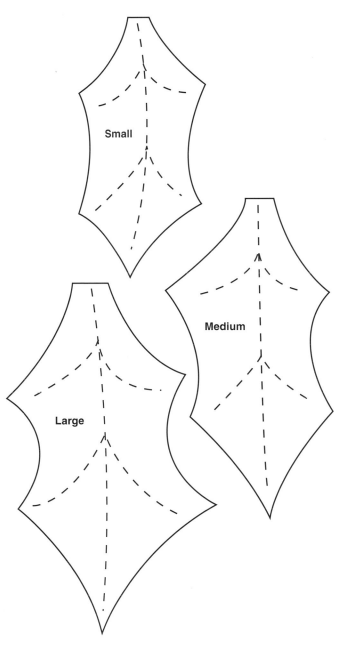

Poinsettia Warmers Templates
Enlarge 200%.

Christmas Carryall

Design by Linda Turner Griepentrog

Carrying all those presents over the river and through the woods to Grandmother's house just got easier. Tuck all those carefully wrapped packages into this sturdy oversized tote for safe transport to any holiday party or get-together.

Finished Size
24 x 15 x 8 inches

Materials
- 44/45-inch-wide cotton fabric:
    - 3/8 yard green holiday print
    - 1/2 yard red-and-green vertical stripe
    - 3/8 yard green solid fabric
    - 1/2 yard red solid poplin (it must be opaque so that other fabrics won't show through)
- 1 yard 60-inch-wide heavyweight white cotton duck or canvas
- 2 1/4 yards 18-inch-wide paper-backed fusible web
- 2 3/4 yards 2-inch-wide white polyester or nylon webbing
- 2 3/4 yards 1-inch-wide red polyester or nylon webbing
- 3 1/4 yards double-fold bias tape
- Monofilament thread
- 8 x 24-inch piece 1/8-inch-thick white fiberboard
- Basic sewing tools and equipment

Cutting
- From the white cotton duck, cut one tote base using the pattern in Figure 1 on page 12.
- From the stripe fabric, cut two 17 x 22-inch rectangles.
- From the holiday print, cut two 11 1/4 x 17-inch rectangles.
- From the green solid fabric, cut one 9 x 18-inch rectangle for the pocket.
- From the red solid fabric, cut one piece 16 x 34 inches.
- From each color of the webbing, cut two 48-inch-long pieces.

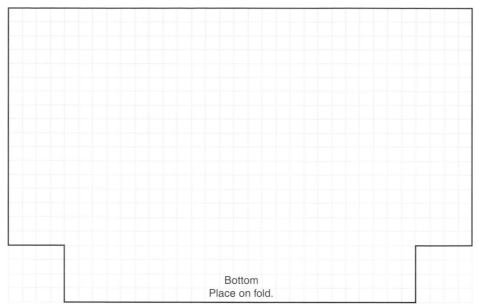

Figure 1
1 square = 1"

Assembly

Note: Use ¼-inch-wide seam allowances.

1. Trim the fusible web to 17 inches wide and cover the tote base front and back sections as shown in Figure 2.

Figure 2
Apply fusible web to right side of tote front/back.

2. Position one holiday stripe and one holiday print section on the fusible-web side of the tote base front and back, overlapping the inner edges ¹⁄₁₆ inch. Follow the manufacturer's instructions to fuse the fabrics in place, making sure they are wrinkle-free (Figure 3). Allow to cool and trim any overhanging edges to match the tote base edges.

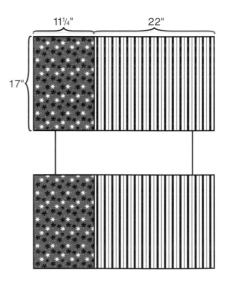

Figure 3
Fuse fabric in place, lapping inner edges.

3. Fold the green pocket rectangle in half with wrong sides facing to create a 9-inch-square double-layer pocket. Cut and insert one 8¾-inch square of fusible web between the layers. Fuse. Mark the pocket center points at the upper and lower edge with a pin.

4. Center the pocket on the tote front with the upper folded edge 5 inches below the tote upper raw edge; baste the side and lower edges in place (Figure 4).

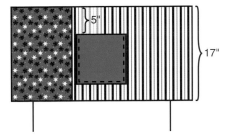

Figure 4
Baste pocket to tote front.

5. Center the red webbing on the white webbing and stitch in place along both long edges using the monofilament thread.

6. Pin the webbing over the pocket on the tote front as shown in Figure 5, overlapping the pocket edges by ½ inch.

Figure 5
Position strap over pocket edges.

7. Edgestitch the webbing in place, stopping 2 inches from the upper tote edge. Pivot and stitch across the white portion of the web, backstitching across the stitching to the edge to reinforce (Figure 6). If desired, change the top thread to red and stitch across the red portion of the strap.

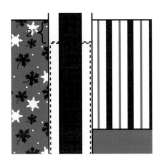

Figure 6
Edgestitch strap in place.

8. Center the webbing on the tote back as shown in Figure 7 and stitch in place as directed above.

Figure 7
Stitch webbing to tote back.

9. Turn under and press ¼ inch along the long edges of the red rectangle for the tote bottom. Fold the strip in half with turned edges even and cut out the corners as shown in Figure 8.

Figure 8
Cut away shaded corners.

10. Pin the red panel to the right side of the tote bottom with raw edges even. Stitch close to the turned edges and ⅛ inch from the raw edges in the cutout areas (Figure 9).

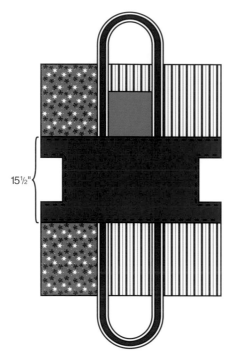

15½"

Figure 9
Center tote bottom panel so it covers web ends and pocket lower edge.

11. Fold the tote in half with right sides facing and stitch the side seams using ⅜-inch-wide seam allowances (Figure 10). To finish the raw edges, bind them as one with the double-fold bias tape. Pin-mark the bottom fold on each side edge.

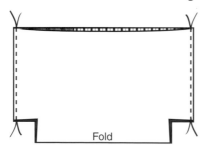

Fold

Figure 10
Stitch side seams.

12. With right sides together and the centers matching the seam line, pin and stitch each corner to box the bottom (Figure 11). Finish with binding, serging or zigzagging. Turn right side out.

Figure 11
Align seam with center and stitch to box the bottom corner.

13. Finish the upper raw edge of the tote with double-fold binding, and then turn under and press a 1½-inch-wide hem. Be careful not to touch the iron to the webbing because it may melt, depending on the fiber content. Hand- or machine-stitch the hem edge in place or use narrow strips of fusible web to adhere the layers for a no-sew finish. ✦

Christmas Countdown

Design by Carol Zentgraf

Make a fun felt Advent calendar to help the wee ones count the days until Christmas. Twenty-four pockets hold machine-embroidered "ornaments." Each is backed with hook tape that adheres to the felt tree as they are added, day by day. Substitute ready-made seasonal appliqués or holiday buttons attached to fabric scraps if an embroidery machine is not available.

Finished Size
24 x 34 inches

Materials
- 1½ yards 45-inch-wide green felt
- ¾ yard 45-inch-wide red felt
- 1 yard 45-inch-wide white or off-white polyester organza for embroideries
- ⅓ yard 1⅜-inch-wide ribbon for hanger
- Machine-embroidery designs for 25 small holiday motifs (Cactus Punch Christmas Holidays 3 Advent Calendar shown)
- Assorted colors rayon machine-embroidery thread
- Bobbin thread for embroidery
- 1 yard fusible structural stabilizer (heavyweight nonwoven)
- Water-soluble stabilizer for machine embroidery
- ⅓ yard fusible hook-and-loop tape (designed for fabric)
- 1½-inch-high iron-on numbers
- Pattern tracing cloth or paper
- Self-adhesive, double-sided basting tape
- Permanent fabric adhesive
- Rotary cutter with wave blade
- Basic sewing tools and equipment

Cutting

- Enlarge the tree pattern on page 19 as directed onto pattern tracing cloth or paper.
- From the green felt, cut two trees and two 2 x 24-inch pocket strips. Trim one long edge of each pocket strip using the rotary cutter with wave blade.
- From the red felt, cut two 10 x 24-inch rectangles and two 2 x 24-inch pocket strips.
- Stack the 10 x 24-inch rectangles with edges even and trim one long edge using the rotary cutter with wave blade, cutting through both layers. Trim one long edge of each pocket strip with the rotary cutter wave blade.
- Trace the tree on the structural stabilizer and cut out ¼ inch inside the drawn lines. Cut one 9½ x 23½-inch rectangle from the stabilizer.

Assembly

1. Center the structural stabilizer tree on one felt tree and fuse in place. Do the same with one red rectangle and the rectangle of stabilizer.

2. To assemble the tree, layer the felt trees with the stabilizer sandwiched between them, and the felt edges aligned. Topstitch the trees together ¼ inch from the outer edge.

3. To assemble the base, layer the red rectangles with the stabilizer sandwiched between and the felt edges aligned. Topstitch the rectangles together ¼ inch from the edges.

4. Apply basting tape along the upper edge of the red felt base. Remove the paper backing. Lap the bottom edge of the tree over the edge of the base and adhere to the basting tape. Stitch in place along the first stitching at the base of the tree (Figure 1).

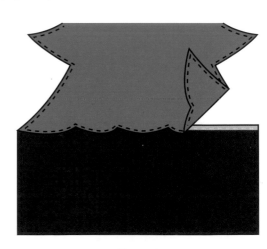

Figure 1
Adhere tree to basting tape on base.

5. Divide and chalk-mark each pocket strip into six 4-inch-wide increments. Center the numbers 1–24 on the marked sections and fuse in place, following the manufacturer's directions.

6. Apply basting tape to the straight long edge and both short edges of each pocket strip and remove the paper backing. With the wavy edges toward the top, adhere the pockets in place. Pin through all layers across each marked section line.

7. Stitching from the lower edge of the base toward the tree, stitch the pockets in place along each marked section line. Topstitch the lower and side edges of the pockets in place ¼ inch from the edges (Figure 2).

Note: Stitching in this order helps prevent the felt strips from stretching as you work.

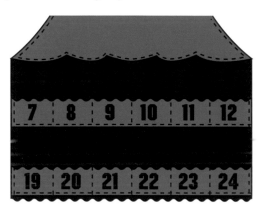

Figure 2
Adhere pocket strips and stitch in place on marked lines and at side and lower edges.

8. Cut the ribbon into three equal lengths. Fold each length in half to make a loop and glue the ends together with permanent fabric adhesive. Glue the base of one loop to the top of the tree, with the loop extending above the tree. Glue the two remaining loops to the upper corners of the base, with the top of the loops just below the edge of the base.

9. Cut pieces of organza large enough to hoop in the embroidery hoop of your machine. Hoop with a layer of water-soluble stabilizer underneath and embroider several motifs on each piece, allowing ½ inch of space around each one. You will need a total of 24 motifs for the pockets, plus an angel or star for the treetop.

10. Remove the embroidered fabric from the hoop and then remove the water-soluble stabilizer following the manufacturer's directions. Allow the embroidered pieces to dry, and then cut around each motif a scant ¼ inch from the outer edge.

11. From the hook half of the hook-and-loop tape, cut 24 pieces each ½ inch long. Remove the backing from each piece and adhere a piece to the wrong side of each motif. Press the motifs from the right side to fuse the tape in place.

12. Attach one embroidered motif to the top of the tree by adhering the tape to the felt. Insert the remaining motifs in the pockets so that a portion of each one shows above the pocket edge.

13. Optional: If desired, tuck a small trinket or a piece of candy in each pocket, too. ✦

Christmas Countdown Pattern
Enlarge 400%.

Pinwheel Candies

Designs by Pam Archer

Candy-themed Christmas decor does a lot to set the mood of this fun-filled, festive season. These felt candy look-alikes are easy to make in the twinkle of an eye. So while you're at it, sew up extras as hostess gifts or for small-gift exchanges. Why stop at one piece of candy when these are guaranteed calorie-free?

Finished Sizes
Gift Bag: 4 x 10 inches
Ornament: 4 inches in diameter
Garland: Approximately 69 inches long

Materials for All Projects
- Template plastic and pencil
- Air-soluble marking pen
- All-purpose thread to match fabrics
- Basic sewing tools and equipment

Gift Bag

Materials
- ⅓ yard bright pink felt
- ⅓ yard olive green felt
- 9 x 16-inch piece lightweight fusible interfacing
- Rotary cutter, mat and ruler

Cutting
- From each color of felt, cut four 5 x 11 rectangles, one 5-inch square and one 2 x 13-inch strip.
- From the fusible interfacing, cut one 5-inch square and one 2 x 13-inch strip.

Assembly
Note: *Use ½-inch-wide seam allowances.*

1. Beginning and ending the stitching precisely ½ inch from each end, stitch a pink rectangle to one side of the pink square (Figure 1 on page 22). Repeat for the remaining sides of square. Press all seams open and trim the seam allowances to ¼ inch.

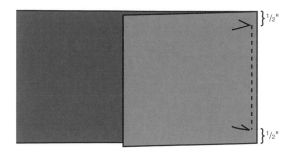

Figure 1
Stitch square to rectangle.

2. Pin and sew the long sides of the rectangles together all around. Press seams open and trim. Turn the bag right side out. Turn under and press ½ inch at the upper edge (Figure 2).

Figure 2
Sew long edges together. Turn under ½" at upper edge.

3. Following the manufacturer's directions, apply the fusible interfacing to the wrong side of the green felt square and the wrong side of one of the strips for the handle. Set the handle aside.

4. Assemble the green bag for the lining in the same manner as for the pink bag, sewing rectangles to side of square without fusible interfacing. Do not turn the lining right side out. Turn ½ inch of upper edge to the wrong side and press.

5. Tuck the lining into the pink bag with wrong sides facing.

6. Turn under and press ½ inch on each long edge of each handle strip. Pin handles, wrong sides together, and stitch close to long edges. Tuck the raw ends of the handle between the bag and lining layers, centering each end between seam allowances on opposite sides of the bag; pin. Edgestitch through all layers (Figure 3).

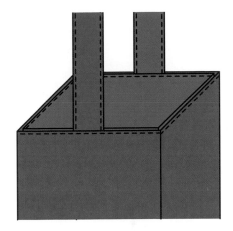

Figure 3
Tuck strap ends between bag and lining; edgestitch.

7. Optional: Make an ornament (see Ornament directions on this page) to tie to one handle of the bag if desired.

Ornaments

Materials for Set of Two Ornaments
• 9 x 12-inch piece bright pink felt
• 5 x 10-inch rectangle cranberry felt
• 5 x 10-inch rectangle olive green felt
• 6 x 12-inch piece lightweight double-sided fusible
   nonwoven interfacing
• ⅓ yard pink rattail cord
• 6-inch-long piece cranberry cord
• 6-inch-long piece green cord

Cutting
• Trace the large circle and pinwheel templates on
   page 25 onto template plastic and cut out.
• Trace four circles on the pink felt and cut out.
• Trace one pinwheel on the cranberry felt and
   one on the olive green felt. Cut out.
• Trace two circles onto the interfacing and cut
   out ⅛ inch inside the traced line.
• Cut two 6-inch lengths of pink cord.

Assembly
1. Pair one pink and one green cord and twist together. Pin to the wrong side of one ornament circle and stitch across the ends. Repeat with the pink and cranberry cords. On each of the two remaining pink circles, position a pinwheel and edgestitch in place (Figure 4).

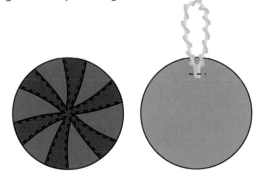

Figure 4
Stitch pinwheel to one circle and twisted cord to other.

2. Sandwich a circle of double-sided fusible interfacing between each pair of circles. Fuse together following the manufacturer's directions. Edgestitch ⅛ inch from the outer edge through all layers.

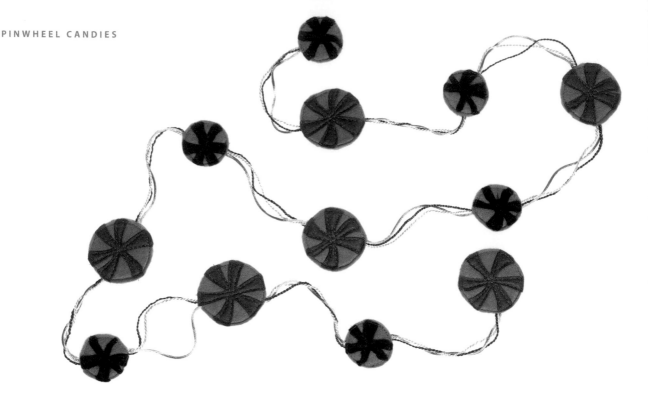

Garland

Materials
- ¼ yard bright pink felt
- 9 x 12-inch piece cranberry felt
- 9 x 12-inch piece green felt
- 8 x 11-inch piece lightweight double-sided fusible nonwoven interfacing
- 2 yards each pink, green and cranberry rattail or other decorative cord

Cutting
- Trace the small and medium circle and pinwheel templates on page 25 onto template plastic and cut out.
- Trace 12 each of the medium and small garland circles onto the pink felt and cut out.
- Trace six each of the medium pinwheels onto the olive green felt. Trace six each of the small pinwheels onto the cranberry felt. Cut out.
- Trace six each of the medium and small circles onto the interfacing and cut out each one ⅛ inch inside the drawn lines.
- Cut one 70-inch length of each cord.

Assembly
1. Tie the cords together at each end with an overhand knot.

2. Position a pinwheel on six of each color and size of the pink circles and edgestitch in place.

3. Working on a large surface, arrange the medium and small circles along the cord at 5-inch intervals with the cord centered and the knots at each end centered on an end circle. Pin in place and then stitch across the cords at each edge of each circle (Figure 5).

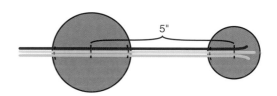

Figure 5
Space large and small circles at 5" intervals, center to center. Stitch at edges.

4. At the ironing board, position the garland cord side up and add an interfacing circle of the appropriate size, followed by a pinwheel circle face up. Fuse in place. Continue in this manner until all layers are fused together.

5. Edgestitch around each circle through all layers. ✦

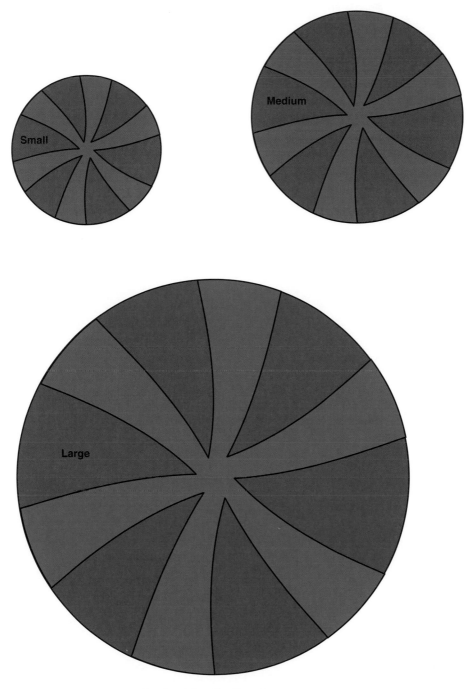

Pinwheel Candies Templates
Actual Size

Jingle Bell Cards

Design by Janis Bullis

Tuck treasured holiday greetings in the pockets of this colorful card holder. Jingle bells and a turned-up toe add to the merriment. Use off-beat colors or more traditional ones to suit your mood.

Finished Size
14 x 32 inches, excluding hanger

Materials
- 1 yard bright green felt
- ⅜ yard bright pink felt
- 4 (9 x 12-inch) rectangles white felt
- 18 (⅜-inch-diameter) jingle bells
- 1 (½-inch-diameter) jingle bell
- All-purpose thread to match felt
- Chalk marker
- Pattern tracing paper or cloth
- Rotary cutter, mat and ruler
- Basic sewing tools and equipment

Cutting
- Enlarge the pattern pieces on page 29 and cut out of pattern tracing paper or cloth.
- From the green felt, cut two stockings, two upper pockets and one lower pocket. Cut two 1½ x 8-inch strips for the hanger.
- From the pink felt, cut three upper pockets.
- From the white felt, cut seven cuffs.

Assembly
1. Measuring from the upper edge, mark pocket placement lines on one green stocking as shown in Figure 1.

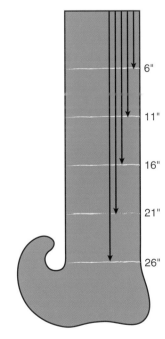

Figure 1
Mark placement lines on one stocking.

2. With the longest straight edges even, stitch one cuff to each of two green and two pink upper pockets and to the green lower pocket ½ inch from the upper raw edges (Figure 2). Using rotary-cutting tools, trim to ¼ inch from the stitching edge.

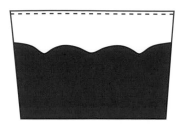

Figure 2
Stitch cuff to 2 pink and 2 green upper pocket pieces. Trim seam to ¼".

3. Pin the longest straight edge of the remaining pink pocket and one cuff even with the upper edge of the marked stocking. Stitch ½ inch from the upper edge. Do not trim the upper edge yet, but do trim the edges of the pocket and cuff even with the side edges of the stocking. Machine-baste a scant ¼ inch from the side edges and stitch ½ inch from the lower raw edge (Figure 3).

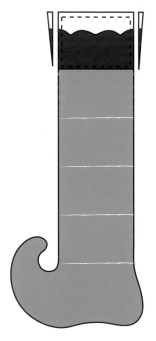

Figure 3
Sew pocket and cuff to upper edge.

4. Pin the remaining cuff to the upper edge on the right side of the remaining green stocking. Make sure the two stockings are mirror images so the cuffs will show on the front and back of the assembled stocking. Stitch ½ inch from the upper raw edges. Trim and stitch the sides as described for the stocking front.

5. Position the remaining pockets on the stocking front along the marked pocket placement lines and pin in place with side raw edges even. Note that the pockets are slightly larger than the stocking so there is room to tuck cards inside. Stitch ½ inch from the lower raw edges (Figure 4). Add the lower pocket to the stocking with raw edges even and machine-baste a scant ¼ inch from the raw edges.

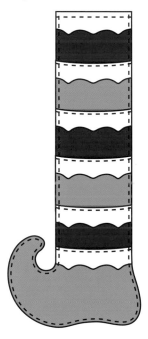

Figure 4
Pin and stitch the pockets to the stocking front.

6. With right sides facing, pin and stitch the pocketed stocking to the remaining stocking along the long edges and around the foot and toe. Stitch ½ inch from the raw edges and trim the seam allowance to ¼ inch. Turn right side out and press the outer edge as needed. Trim the upper edge of the stocking front and back ¼ inch from the stitching.

7. Layer the strips for the hanger with wrong sides facing and stitch ½ inch from each long edge. Trim to ¼ inch from each row of stitching. Fold the strip in half to create a hanging loop. Tuck the ends between the stocking layers and pin. Stitch through all layers across the upper edge, catching the hanger in the stitching.

8. Hand-sew a small jingle bell to each point on every cuff. Sew the large bell to the toe. ✦

Lower Pocket

Stocking

Cuff

Upper Pocket

Jingle Bell Cards Patterns
Enlarge 400%.

Sock-It-to-Me Knit Wits

Designs by Linda Turner Griepentrog

Turn a thrift-store sweater and tie into a clever stocking for Santa to fill with Christmas goodies. Or recycle a colorful pullover that you or another family member may no longer wear into a fun-to-wear stocking hat. Recycling puts a holiday spin on these sew-to-save gifts to give.

Finished Sizes
Shirt & Tie Required: 11 x 18 inches
Hat Trick: Your size (adult or child)

Shirt & Tie Required

Materials
- Lightweight collared, button-front knit sweater
- Necktie (knitted, as shown, or silk)
- Fabric belt with a usable buckle portion approximately 13 inches long
- ⅜ yard 44/45-inch-wide tartan plaid for lining
- Lightweight polyester batting
- All-purpose thread to match sweater
- Pattern tracing paper or cloth
- Temporary spray adhesive
- Chalk marker
- Basic sewing tools and equipment

Cutting
- Carefully remove the center back label in the sweater and then button the front placket. Set the label aside to reattach later if desired.
- Turn the sweater wrong side out and fold carefully along the shoulder seams, smoothing the collar in place inside.
- Enlarge the pattern on page 34 on pattern tracing paper or cloth and cut out. Position the pattern on the sweater as shown in Figure 1 on page 32, making sure the pattern is positioned so the toe of the finished stocking will point in the desired direction when turned right side out. Cut through both layers of the sweater on the long and curved edges of the pattern. *Do not cut along the upper edge (neckline with collar).*
- From the lining fabric, cut one 13 x 40-inch rectangle. Repeat with the batting.

Figure 1
Align stocking pattern with sweater shoulders on wrong side.

Assembly

1. Refer to Figure 2 for steps 1–3. Apply a light coat of spray adhesive to the wrong side of the lining rectangle and smooth in place on the batting. Apply spray adhesive to the exposed side of the batting and smooth the sweater stocking in place on top. Chalk-mark toe and heel quilting lines ¼ inch apart on the sock front only.

2. Adjust the machine for a long basting stitch and stitch through all layers along the toe and heel quilting lines.

3. Trim the excess batting and lining along the stocking outer raw edges and ¼ inch inside the neckline edge to allow for finishing (Figure 2).

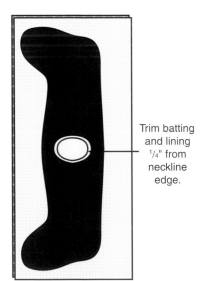

Trim batting and lining ¹⁄₄" from neckline edge.

Figure 2
Layer lining, batting and stocking.

4. Turn under the raw edges of the lining/batting layer and pin around the neckline, covering the collar seam. Slipstitch in place and then reattach the sweater label if desired (Figure 3).

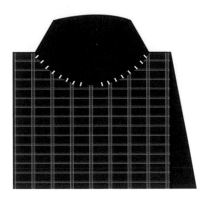

Figure 3
Turn under and slipstitch lining/batting to neckline stitching line around lower edge of collar.

5. Fold the belt in half with wrong sides together and baste the cut ends together. Position on the stocking front at an angle and baste in place (Figure 4).

Figure 4
Baste folded belt to stocking front at hanging angle.

6. With right sides facing, fold the stocking at the shoulder seams and stitch ½ inch from the outer edge. Trim to ¼ inch and zigzag-finish or serge the layers together (Figure 5).

Figure 5
Stitch stocking perimeter and finish edges.

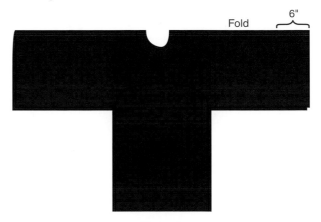

Figure 1
Measure and mark hat-cutting line on folded sweater.

underarm seams and fold with right sides together along a knit rib at the center front and back (see Figure 1).

7. Turn the stocking right side out through the neck opening. Tack the center back of the collar over the seam line, insert the tie and knot in place. Depending on the weight of the sweater knit, it may be necessary to invisibly tack the collar in place over the tie. Add a tie tack, if desired, to hold the tie in place.

Note: If the tie is too long for the stocking, wrap it twice around the neckline, or cut and seam it at the center back to shorten it. The seam will be hidden under the collar.

Hat Trick

Materials
• Adult-size pullover sweater with ribbed
    lower edge
• Contrasting worsted weight yarn
• Coordinating serger/sewing thread
• Chalk marker
• 3 x 6-inch piece cardboard
• Tapestry needle
• Basic sewing tools and equipment

Cutting
• Cut the sweater open along the side and sleeve

• Measure the circumference of your head and subtract 1 inch. Measure half this distance along the lower ribbed edge of one folded sweater section, being careful not to stretch the ribbing; place a pin at the mark.
• Determine the maximum allowable length for the hat and measure up the center fold, staying clear of any neckline opening trim.

Note: For the longest possible hat, measure and mark the hat cutting lines on the sweater back, since it is longer than the front due to a higher neckline in back.

• Chalk-mark a line from the pin straight up 6 inches; then taper to the desired length (Figure 1 above). If desired, mark and cut a second hat from the remaining half of the sweater.
• Cut along the line and carefully move the knit shape to the sewing machine.
• From the remainder of the sweater, cut a 4-inch-wide piece for the cuff that is 2 inches smaller than the measurement across the lower edge of the hat along the bottom of the ribbing. This piece will include some ribbing and some of the

remainder of the sweater so you must measure the 4 inches of width from the lower edge of the ribbing into the body of the sweater. You will stretch it slightly when sewing it to the lower edge of the hat.

Assembly

Note: Use ¼-inch-wide seam allowances.

1. Serge or straight-stitch the hat back seam line, matching the lower ribbed edges and any crosswise patterning. To finish a straight-stitched seam, zigzag next to it to prevent raveling. Turn the hat right side out and gently poke out the point.

2. With right sides facing, fold the cuff in half and stitch the short ends together.

3. With the right side of the cuff against the wrong side of the hat and seam matching, serge the two layers together, slightly stretching the cuff to fit. Turn the cuff to the right side of the hat, hiding the seam.

4. To make the pompom, wrap the yarn around the cardboard rectangle length until you are satisfied with the fullness.

5. Slide the yarn off the cardboard and tie securely with matching yarn at the center, leaving 8-inch-long yarn tails. Clip the yarn loops at each end, if desired, or leave them unclipped (Figure 2).

Figure 2
Wrap yarn on cardboard, slide off and tie center.

6. Thread the yarn ends into a tapestry needle and sew the pompom through the hat point. Anchor the yarn ends securely on the inside of the hat point. ✦

Shirt & Tie Required Pattern
Englarge 400%.

Pet Hang-Ups

Designs by Carol Zentgraf

Gift your four-legged friends all year long with these clever "Christmas" stockings. Stitched in non-Christmasy colors, you can use them for any season and any reason. Your pets will tune in to the jingle-bell bows and know treats are in store when you hang them with care at the mantel or elsewhere.

Finished Sizes
Bone Stocking: 11 x 17 inches
Fish Stocking: 9 x 17 inches

Materials for One Stocking (Bone or Fish)
- ½ yard each 2 coordinating cotton prints for "stocking" and lining
- 1-inch-diameter circle black felt for fish eye
- 6-inch-long piece ¼-inch-wide coordinating satin ribbon for hanging loop
- 2 yards 3-inch-wide sheer ribbon for bow
- Pattern tracing cloth or paper
- All-purpose thread to match fabrics
- 2 (¾-inch-diameter) jingle bells
- Permanent fabric adhesive
- Basic sewing tools and equipment

Cutting
- Enlarge the patterns on page 39 onto pattern tracing cloth or paper and cut out.
- Use the pattern to cut two identical pieces from the fabric for the stocking and for the lining—a total of four pieces for one stocking.
- From sheer ribbon, cut two 1-yard lengths.

Assembly
Note: *Use ⅜-inch-wide seam allowances.*

1. For the stocking, with right sides facing sew the bone or fish shapes together, leaving the upper edge open as shown in Figure 1 on page 38. Turn right side out and press. Trim the seams to ¼ inch.

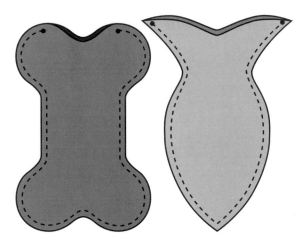

Figure 1
Sew shapes together for outer
stocking, leaving upper edge open.

2. Sew the lining pieces together in the same
manner, leaving the upper edge open as for the
outer stocking, plus a 4-inch-long opening in
one straight edge of the bone or along one edge
above the point in the fish opening in the lower
edge (Figure 2). Trim the seams to ¼ inch wide.
Do not turn the lining right side out.

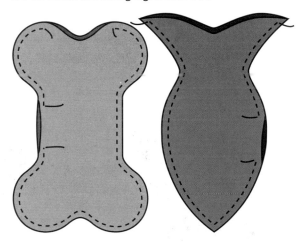

Figure 2
Sew lining pieces together. Leave top
open and opening at side edge for turning.

3. With right sides facing and side seams aligned,
place the outer stocking inside the lining. Pin the
upper raw edges together on each half of the
opening and stitch around the opening. You will

need to begin and end the stitching at the dots on
each half, connecting the new stitching with the
previous stitching (Figure 3).

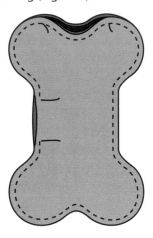

Figure 3
Sew stocking to lining at upper opening edges.

4. To turn right side out, pull the outer stocking
through the opening in the lining and turn the
lining right side out. Turn in the opening edges
and press, and then topstitch the layers together,
close to the turned edges.

5. Tuck the lining inside the stocking and press the
opening edges as needed. Fold the satin ribbon in
half to form a loop and tuck between the layers at
one corner of the opening. Pin in place. Topstitch
¼ inch from the finished edges, backstitching over
the ribbon loop (Figure 4).

Figure 4
Tuck ribbon ends between layers. Topstitch
around outer edge; catch ribbon in stitching.

6. Layer the two lengths of sheer ribbon with long edges even. Tie into a bow with streamers, adjusting as needed to fit across the upper stocking and using permanent fabric adhesive to attach the bow to the stocking. Use a small spot of glue under the bow ends to secure them. Trim the tails to the desired length; gather each short end with hand stitching so that you can tuck the end into the loop on a jingle bell and hand-sew securely in place.

7. For the fish stocking, use permanent fabric adhesive to secure the 1-inch-diameter black felt circle to the front of the stocking for the fish eye. ✦

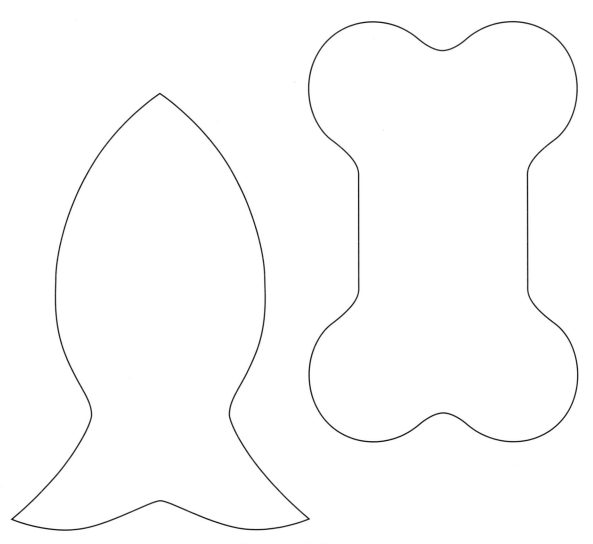

Fish & Bone Patterns
Enlarge 400%.

Mitten Gift Bags

Designs by Angie Wilhite

These little gift bags can do double duty as ornaments for your tree or fireplace mantel. Hand stitching and buttons are easy-to-sew embellishments.

Finished Sizes

Snowman Sam: 4½ x 7½ inches, excluding hanging loop
Perky Penguin: 4½ x 8½ inches, excluding hanging loop
Reindeer Merrymaker: 4½ x 9 inches, excluding hanging loop

Materials for All Mittens

• Template plastic or pattern tracing paper
• Press cloth or appliqué pressing sheet
• All-purpose thread to match buttons
• Basic hand-sewing tools

Snowman Sam

Materials

• 10-inch square blue wool felt
• 6 x 8-inch piece cream wool felt
• 2-inch square orange wool felt
• 8-inch square lightweight paper-backed fusible web
• ³⁄₁₆-inch-diameter buttons: 2 black, 1 green, 1 brown and 1 burgundy

• 2 (⅝-inch-diameter) natural wooden buttons
• 6-strand embroidery floss: black and cream

Note: Cover all felt pieces with appliqué pressing sheet or press cloth before fusing.

Assembly

1. Trace the mitten and loop shapes on page 44 onto template plastic or pattern tracing paper and cut out. Cut two mittens from blue felt and position with raw edges even all around.

2. Using 2 strands of cream embroidery floss, blanket stitch across the upper edge of one layer of the mitten front. Continue blanket stitching around both layers to complete the mitten construction.

3. For loop, cut two 1½ x 6½-inch strips of blue felt and one strip of fusible web.

4. Trace the loop shape on the paper side of the fusible strip. Following manufacturer's instructions, apply the fusible web to one blue strip. Cut out on the traced lines.

5. Remove the backing paper. Fuse the strip to the remaining blue strip following the manufacturer's directions. Cut away the excess around the loop shape.

6. Using 2 strands of cream embroidery floss, blanket-stitch around the loop edges.

7. Wrap the loop ends around the upper left corner of the mitten and pin in place. Position a wooden button on top and sew in place, using thread to match the button and sewing through all thicknesses.

8. From the cream felt, cut two 3 x 4-inch pieces. Cut two 1 x 2-inch orange felt pieces. Trace the snowman and nose pieces onto corresponding pieces of fusible web. Following the manufacturer's directions, apply fusible web to one each of the cream and orange felt pieces. Cut out the shapes on the drawn lines and remove the backing paper.

9. Fuse each piece to the remaining piece of the same color; cut away the excess felt around each piece.

10. Using 2 strands of black embroidery floss, blanket-stitch around the nose and the curved edges of the snowman. Use a scrap of fusible web to fuse the nose to the snowman (see photo). Sew black buttons for eyes to the snowman. Sew the green, brown and burgundy buttons to the center of the snowman.

11. Use a scrap of fusible web to fuse the snowman to the upper right corner of the mitten.

12. Flip the mitten thumb back over the snowman; with the remaining wooden button on top, sew in place through all layers.

Perky Penguin

Materials
- 10-inch square orange wool felt
- 6 x 8-inch piece black wool felt
- 3 x 4-inch piece cream wool felt
- 1 x 3-inch piece dark red wool felt
- 8 x 10-inch piece lightweight paper-backed fusible web
- 1/8-inch-diameter buttons: 2 black and 1 green
- 2 (5/8-inch-diameter) natural wooden buttons
- All-purpose thread to match dark red felt
- 6-strand embroidery floss: black and cream

Assembly
1. Cut the mitten pieces from orange felt and construct the mitten following steps 2–7 for Snowman Sam.

2. Cut two 3 x 4-inch pieces from black felt.

3. On the paper side of the fusible web, trace the two penguin shapes and the beak, leaving at least 1/4 inch of space between the pieces. Cut apart, leaving a 1/8-inch margin beyond the drawn lines. Apply the pieces to the appropriate-color pieces of felt, following the manufacturer's directions.

4. Cut out each shape on the lines and remove the backing paper. Fuse to the remaining piece of matching felt. Trim away the excess felt beyond the upper layer edges.

5. Fuse the cream shape to the black penguin shape. Add the beak and fuse in place. Using 2 strands of black embroidery floss, blanket-stitch around the beak and the curved edges of the penguin. Sew on black buttons for eyes above beak.

6. Cut a 3/4 x 2-inch strip of dark red felt for the bow tie. With needle and knotted thread, hand-baste across the center of the felt strip. Draw up the thread to gather and knot. Attach the bow tie to the penguin by sewing the green button in place at the center through all layers.

7. Complete the gift bag following steps 11 and 12 for Snowman Sam.

Reindeer Merrymaker

Materials

- 10-inch square dark red wool felt
- 6 x 8-inch piece tan wool felt
- 5 x 8-inch piece brown wool felt
- 4-inch square green wool felt
- 7-inch-square lightweight paper-backed fusible web
- ⅛-inch-diameter buttons: 2 black and 1 red
- 2 (⅝-inch diameter) natural wooden buttons
- 6-strand embroidery floss: black and cream

Assembly

1. Cut the mitten pieces from dark red felt and construct the mitten following steps 2–7 for Snowman Sam.

2. Cut two 3 x 4-inch pieces from the tan felt for the reindeer and two 4 x 5-inch brown felt pieces for the antlers. Cut two 2 x 4-inch pieces of green felt for the holly leaves and a 1-inch square of dark red felt for the nose.

3. Trace the reindeer, antlers, two holly leaves and the nose onto the paper side of the fusible web, allowing at least ¼ inch of space between the pieces. Cut out each one with a ⅛-inch-wide margin beyond the lines.

4. Following manufacturer's directions, fuse the pieces to the appropriate-color felt. Remove the backing paper and fuse each piece to the remaining matching piece of felt. Cut away the excess felt around each piece.

5. Using 2 strands of black embroidery floss, blanket-stitch around the curved edges of the reindeer. Position the nose on the reindeer and fuse in place. Using 2 strands of black embroidery floss, blanket-stitch around the nose. Sew two black buttons to the reindeer for eyes.

6. Using 2 strands of black embroidery floss, do a running stitch along the center of each holly leaf. Center and sew the red button about ½ inch above the lower edge of the reindeer. Glue the holly leaves in place (see photo).

7. Use a scrap of fusible web to fuse the antlers to the back of the reindeer.

8. Complete the gift bag following steps 11 and 12 for Snowman Sam. ✦

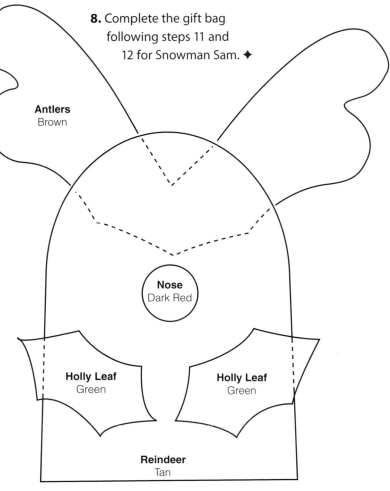

Mitten Gift Bag Template
Actual Size
See assembly directions for special cutting instructions.

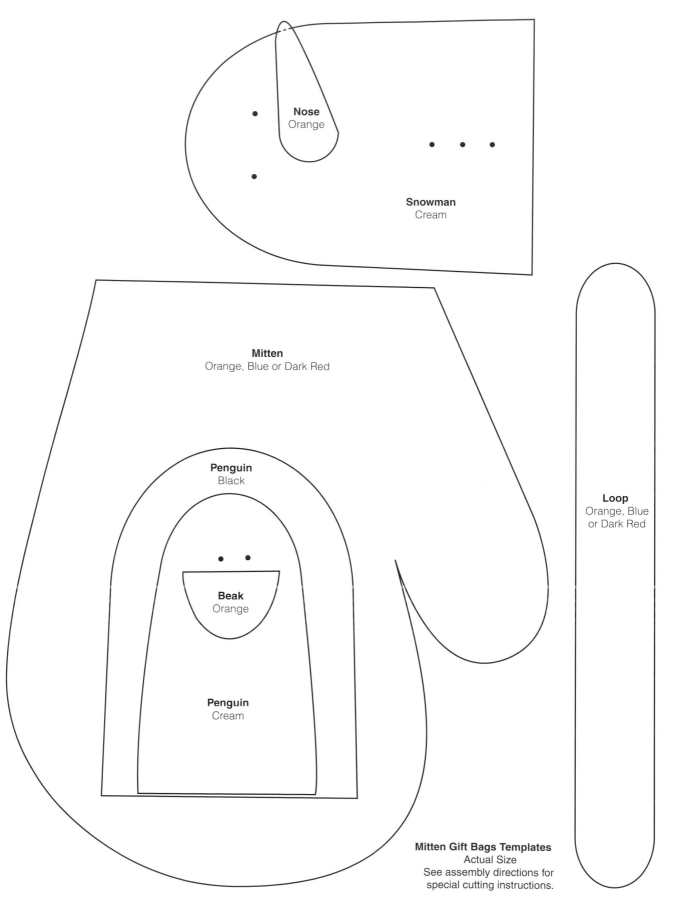

Nose
Orange

Snowman
Cream

Mitten
Orange, Blue or Dark Red

Penguin
Black

Beak
Orange

Penguin
Cream

Loop
Orange, Blue
or Dark Red

Mitten Gift Bags Templates
Actual Size
See assembly directions for
special cutting instructions.

Deck the Halls

No matter what your style, from country to sophisticated, you're sure to find plenty of projects here to inspire your holiday decorating. Make pillows and matching stockings, try a nontraditional color scheme for your tree skirt this year, or make a snowman quilt to snuggle under through the winter.

Hanky-Panky Stockings

Designs by Marta Alto

Make a silk stocking for everyone in the family and use grandma's heirloom hankies for the pretty cuffs. Choose a different-color silk for each person and embellish as desired. Twin-needle stitching, piping and machine embroidery are just a few of the options to consider.

Finished Size
Approximately 16 inches long

Materials for One Stocking
• ½ yard silk dupioni
• ½ yard lightweight fusible interfacing
• ½ yard matching or coordinating lining fabric
• 1½ yards ⅜-inch-diameter cotton cable cord for piping
• 1 vintage or new hanky for the cuff
• 12-inch-long piece ¼- or ½-inch-wide ribbon for hanging loop
• All-purpose thread to match or contrast with fabric as desired
• 24 x 18-inch piece lightweight cotton batting
• Pattern tracing paper or cloth
• Temporary spray adhesive
• Rotary cutter, mat and ruler
• Basic sewing tools and equipment

Cutting
• Enlarge the stocking pattern as directed on page 50 on pattern tracing paper or cloth and cut out.
• Apply fusible interfacing to the wrong side of the silk dupioni following the manufacturer's directions.
• Use the pattern to cut two stockings each from the batting, interfaced silk and lining fabrics. Make sure to cut a front and back from the silk and the lining.
• From the remaining silk fabric, cut three 1¾-inch-wide true-bias strips (enough to make one long strip to fit around the stocking perimeter).

Assembly

Note: Use ½-inch-wide seam allowances.

1. Apply a light coat of temporary spray adhesive to the interfaced side of each stocking and smooth into place on the batting. Quilt the stocking front and/or back if desired. Try twin-needle stitching in a grid or in a serpentine stitch pattern, if available on your machine. Built-in decorative stitches are another option.

2. Sew the bias strips together with bias seams and press the seams open (Figure 1).

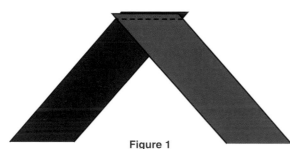

Figure 1
Join strips with bias seams.

3. Attach the zipper foot to the sewing machine and adjust to the right of the needle. Wrap the bias strip around the cotton cable cord with raw edges even and stitch close to the cord (Figure 2).

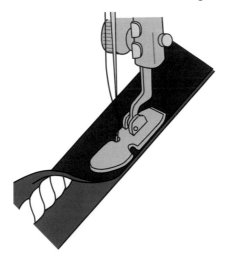

Figure 2
Stitch close to cord.

4. With raw edges even, pin and machine-baste the piping to the outer edge of the stocking front. Use a contrasting thread in the bobbin so the stitching is visible on the wrong side.

5. With right sides facing and the stocking front on top, pin and stitch the stockings together. Stitch just inside the basting. Turn the stocking right side out.

6. With right sides facing, stitch the stocking linings together, leaving a 5-inch-long opening in the back seam for turning later (Figure 3). Do not turn the lining right side out.

Note: Use a ½-inch-wide seam allowance at the beginning and end of the stitching, but increase the seam allowance width to ⅝ inch around the remainder of the lining seam for a better lining fit inside the stocking.

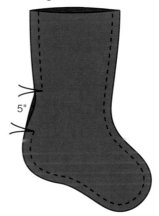

5"

Figure 3
Leave opening in lining for turning.

7. Fold the hanky in half diagonally and cut along the fold. Set half of the hanky aside.

8. Position the hanky at the upper edge of the stocking with the corner centered to form the cuff. Cut away excess hanky. Pin the upper edge of the hanky to the upper edge of the silk stocking. Fold the ribbon in half to create a loop and position at the upper edge at the back seam. Baste in place (Figure 4).

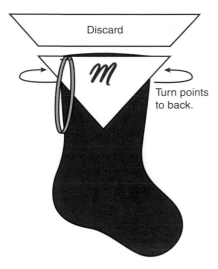

Figure 4
Cut away excess hanky.
Baste hanging loop in place.

9. With right sides facing, tuck the silk stocking inside the lining and pin together at the upper raw edges. Stitch ½ inch from the upper edge. Trim the seam to ¼ inch.

10. Turn the silk stocking right side out through the opening in the lining. Trim and press the opening edges and stitch through all layers close to the edges. Tuck the lining inside the completed stocking. ✦

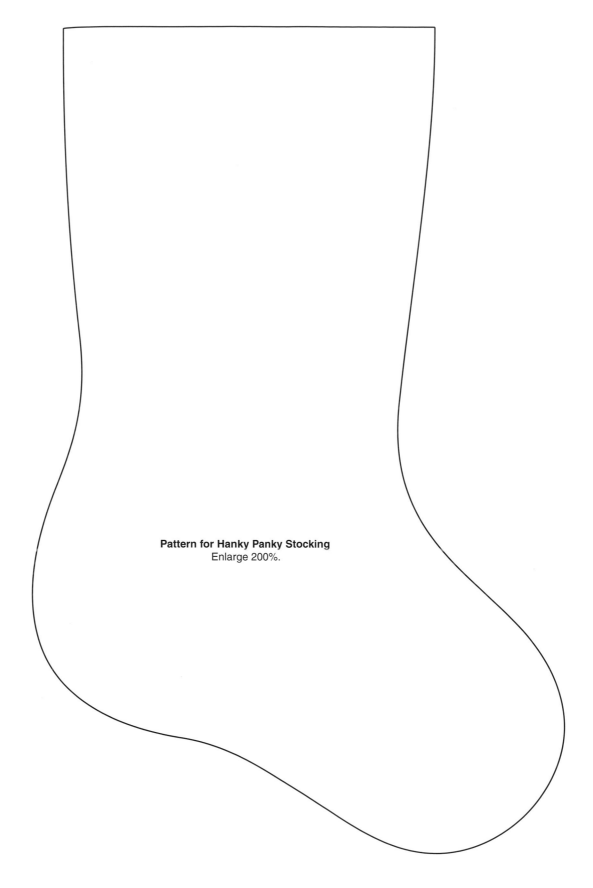

Pattern for Hanky Panky Stocking
Enlarge 200%.

On, Dancer!

Designs by Janis Bullis

Break with tradition and choose an out-of-the-ordinary color scheme for your Christmas decorating this year. Santa's stylized reindeer prance across the midnight sky, all lit up with button stars, on this tree skirt and coordinating throw pillows.

Finished Sizes
Tree Skirt: 50 inches in diameter
Pillow A: 14 inches square
Pillow B: 16 inches square

Tree Skirt

Materials
- 54-inch-wide lightweight plain-weave wool or wool-blend
  - 1½ yards navy
  - 1¾ yards white
- 1 yard (⅛-inch-diameter) rattail cord
- 1¼ yards paper-backed fusible web
- 9 (12-inch) squares iron-on tear-away stabilizer
- All-purpose thread to match fabrics
- 16 (½-inch-diameter) gold star buttons
- 5 (¾-inch-diameter) covered-button forms
- Tape measure
- Tailor's chalk or chalk pencil
- Basic sewing tools and equipment

Cutting
- Fold the navy wool in half lengthwise with selvages even and then fold in half again crosswise, keeping the selvages even. Make sure there are no wrinkles or folds in the fabric layers.
- Using a tape measure as a compass, mark 25 inches from the corner at several locations, moving the tape slightly each time to mark the cutting radius for the skirt. Mark a cutting line 3 inches from the folded corner in the same manner (Figure 1).

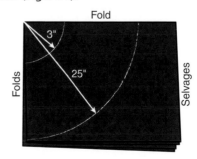

Figure 1
Mark cutting lines on folded wool.

- Cut along the marked lines through all layers to create a 50-inch-diameter circle with a 6-inch-diameter hole in the center. Set the scraps aside for the covered buttons. Unfold the circle halfway and cut along one fold up to the inner cut edge to create the center front opening in the skirt (Figure 2).

Figure 2
Slash along fold to create opening.

- From white wool, cut four 3 x 60-inch true-bias strips for the binding. From the remaining fabric, cut nine 10-inch squares for the appliqués.
- From the paper-backed fusible web, cut nine (9-inch) squares.
- Enlarge the reindeer template on page 56 as directed and trace one onto the paper side of each square of fusible web. Cut out each reindeer along the traced lines.

Tree Skirt Assembly

1. Staystitch ½ inch from the inner circle and the center-front cut edges. On the wrong side of the skirt, mark the center on one edge of the front opening. Using this mark as center, mark the button placements for five button loops, spacing the marks 4 inches apart. Cut five 6-inch-long pieces of rattail cord. Fold each piece in half and position at one of the button-placement marks. Stitch in place ½ inch from the raw edge, backstitching across the cords to secure (Figure 3).

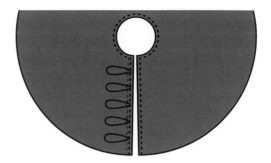

Figure 3
Staystitch ½" from inner circle and opening edges. Position loops and stitch in place.

2. Using bias seams, sew the white wool bias strips together to make one long strip. Press the seams open. Turn under and press ¼ inch at one angled end of the strip.

3. Beginning at the center back of the circle with raw edges even and right sides facing, stitch the binding strip to the outer edge of the skirt ¾ inch from the raw edges. Miter the corners when you reach them by stopping the stitching precisely ¾ inch from the corner; then rotate the piece and create a right-angle fold as shown before continuing the stitching (Figures 4a and 4b).

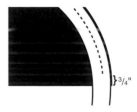

Figure 4a
End stitching precisely ¾" from corner.

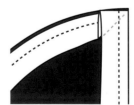

Figure 4b
Make a diagonal fold; then fold binding back on itself.

4. When you reach the beginning of the binding strip, make a neat join and complete the stitching. Wrap the bias to the wrong side of the skirt over the seam allowance. Turn under the raw edge along the stitching, making mitered folds at the corners. Press and then slipstitch in place.

5. Remove the paper backing from each of the nine reindeer appliqués.

6. Fold the skirt in half to locate the center back and mark with a pin or chalk. Center one reindeer appliqué at the mark with the bottom edge of the front hoof 3½ inches from the inner edge of the bias and the back hoof 2½ inches from the inner edge of the bias (Figure 5).

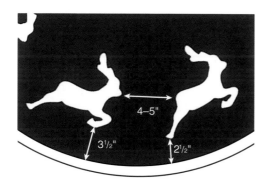

Figure 5
Position and fuse reindeer to tree skirt.

7. Fuse in place. Arrange and pin the remaining reindeer to the tree skirt, allowing 4–5 inches of space between the nose of one and the tail of the next one. Adjust the spacing as needed and then fuse in place following the manufacturer's directions.

8. One by one, satin-stitch the appliqués in place after adjusting your machine for a closely spaced, medium-width stitch and testing it on scraps first. Pivot carefully at the corners on the hooves. To prevent distortion, back each appliqué with a 12-inch square of stabilizer before doing the satin stitching. Remove the stabilizer after completing

the satin stitching and pulling the thread tails to the underside and tying off securely.

9. Make five covered buttons using the navy scraps and following the package directions. Sew in place in the center of the bias trim opposite the rattail loops.

10. Embellish the skirt with gold star buttons as desired.

Pillow A

Materials
- 54-inch-wide lightweight plain-weave wool or wool-blend
  - ½ yard navy
  - ½ yard white
- All-purpose thread to match fabrics
- 9-inch square paper-backed fusible web
- 12-inch square iron-on, tear-away stabilizer
- 3 (½-inch-diameter) gold star buttons
- 2 yards ⅜-inch-diameter filler cord for welting
- 14-inch-square ready-made pillow form
- Basic sewing tools and equipment

Cutting
- From navy wool, cut two 15-inch squares.
- From the white wool, cut one 10-inch square

and two 2⅛ x 40-inch true-bias strips for the welting (piece the strips if necessary)

- Enlarge the reindeer template on page 56 as directed and trace onto the paper side of the fusible web.
- Apply the square of fusible web to the wrong side of the wool square following the manufacturer's directions. Cut out the appliqué along the drawn lines.

Assembly

Note: Use ½-inch-wide seam allowances.

1. Position the appliqué in the center of one 15-inch square of wool and fuse in place. Apply iron-on tear-away stabilizer to the wrong side of the square under the appliqué.

2. Adjust the machine for a satin stitch and test on fabric scraps. Adjust the width and length as necessary to cover the edges of the appliqué. Satin-stitch over the raw edges of the appliqué using white thread in the needle and navy thread in the bobbin. Pivot carefully at corners. Remove the stabilizer from the wrong side. Press.

3. Arrange and stitch three star buttons to pillow front (see pillow photo for placement).

4. Make and apply white welting to the outer edge of the pillow top following the directions for Oh, Welt It! at right.

5. With right sides facing and the pillow front on top, pin the pillow front to the pillow back. Stitch just inside the welting stitching and leave a 10-inch-long opening for turning in the lower edge.

6. Turn the pillow cover right side out and insert the pillow form through the opening. Slipstitch the opening edge to the welting along the seam line.

Oh, Welt It!

1. Sew the bias strips for the welting together using ¼-inch-wide bias seams; press the seams open.

2. Wrap the fabric strip around the filler cord with wrong sides facing.

3. Attach the zipper foot and adjust it to the right of the needle. Machine-baste as close as possible to the cord without catching it in the stitching, leaving a few inches unstitched at each end (Figure 1).

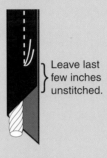

Leave last few inches unstitched.

Figure 1
Wrap cord with fabric and stitch close to cord.

4. Position the raw edges of the welting along the pillow-top raw edge, beginning and ending near the center of the lower edge. Clip the welting seam allowance as needed to ease it around the corners. Machine-baste in place close to the piping stitching, using the zipper foot to stitch close to the cord. Use a contrasting-color thread in the bobbin so you can see the basting on the wrong side. When you reach the beginning point, cut the cord so the two ends butt when the fabric is wrapped around them in the overlap as shown in Figure 2.

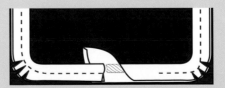

Figure 2
Sew welting to pillow front along first stitching.

Pillow B

Materials

- 54-inch-wide lightweight plain-weave
  wool or wool-blend
    - ¾ yard navy
    - ½ yard white
- 9-inch square paper-backed fusible web
- 12-inch square iron-on, tear-away stabilizer
- 3 (1¼-inch-diameter) covered-button forms

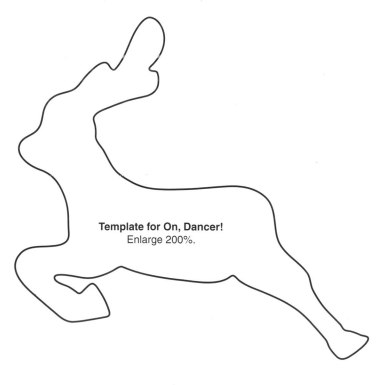

Template for On, Dancer!
Enlarge 200%.

- 2 yards ½-inch-diameter filler cord for welting
- 16-inch-square ready-made pillow form
- All-purpose thread to match fabrics
- Basic sewing tools and equipment

Cutting

- From navy wool, cut two 12 x 17-inch rectangles. From the remaining fabric, cut enough 2¼ inch-wide true-bias strips to make a strip 62 inches long for the welting. Set the remaining fabric scraps aside for the covered buttons.
- From white wool, cut two 6 x 17-inch rectangles and one 10-inch square for the appliqué.
- Enlarge the reindeer template on this page as directed and trace onto the paper side of the fusible web.
- Apply the square of fusible web to the wrong side of the white wool square following the manufacturer's directions. Cut out the appliqué along the drawn lines.

Assembly

Note: *Use ½-inch-wide seam allowances.*

1. With right sides together and long cut edges even, pin and sew each white rectangle to a navy rectangle. Press the seams open.

2. Position the appliqué in the center of the navy section and fuse in place following the manufacturer's directions. Apply iron-on tear-away stabilizer to the wrong side of the pillow front, centering it under the appliqué.

3. Adjust the machine for a satin stitch and test on fabric scraps. Adjust the width and length as necessary to cover the edges of the appliqué. Satin-stitch over the raw edges of the appliqué using white thread in the needle and navy thread in the bobbin. Pivot carefully at corners. Remove the stabilizer from the wrong side. Press.

4. Make and apply welting as directed in Oh, Welt It! on page 55.

5. With right sides facing and the pillow front on top, pin the pillow front to the pillow back. Stitch just inside the welting stitching, leaving a 12-inch-long opening for turning in the lower edge.

6. Turn the pillow cover right side out and insert the pillow form through the opening. Slipstitch the opening edge to the welting along the seam line.

7. Make three navy covered buttons following the package directions. Position one at the center of the white panel and allow 4 inches from shank to shank when positioning and sewing the remaining two buttons in place. ✦

Homespun Christmas

Designs by Lynn Weglarz

Here's a trio of Christmas cheer to stitch for your "country" home, all made from warm and cozy flannel! The mini-stocking ornament would also make a great name tag for Christmas packages.

Finished Sizes
Stocking: 11½ x 18 inches
Pillow: 12 x 16 inches
Ornament: 5½ x 7 inches

Materials for All Projects
• All-purpose thread to match fabrics
• Pattern tracing paper or cloth
• Rotary cutter, mat and ruler
• Basic sewing tools and equipment

Stocking

Materials
• 44/45-inch-wide flannel
    1 yard red for stocking and lining
    ¼ yard green for cuff, heel and toe
    ¼ yard coordinating plaid for cuff and
        prairie points
• ½ yard lightweight batting

• ⅓ yard ¼-inch-wide ribbon or cord for hanger
• Heavyweight black thread for decorative stitching
• 3 (1⅛-inch-diameter) covered-button forms
• Topstitching needle
• Temporary spray adhesive

Cutting
• Enlarge the stocking, toe and heel patterns on page 65 as directed onto pattern tracing paper or cloth and cut out. Use the stocking pattern to cut four stockings from the red flannel for the stocking and lining. Cut two stockings from lightweight batting.
• From the green flannel, cut one each of the toe and heel and two 2¾ x 16-inch strips for the cuff.
• From the plaid flannel, cut two 5¼ x 16-inch strips for the cuff and one 3¼ x 19½-inch strip for the prairie points. From the prairie-point strip, cut six 3¼-inch squares.

Assembly

Note: Use ½-inch-wide seam allowances unless otherwise directed.

1. Apply a light coat of spray adhesive to one side of each piece of batting and smooth a red stocking in place on top. Machine-baste ¼ inch from the raw edges.

2. Position the heel and toe on the right side of one batting-backed stocking and pin in place. Adjust the machine for a blanket or appliqué stitch, insert the topstitching needle and thread the needle with the heavyweight black thread. Stitch the pieces in place along the inner curved edges.

3. With right sides facing, stitch the stocking front to the remaining batting-backed stocking, leaving the upper edge open. Trim the seam to ¼ inch and clip the curves as needed. Turn the stocking right side out. With right sides facing and using a ½-inch-wide seam allowance so the lining will fit smoothly inside the stocking, sew the remaining red flannel stockings together; leave the upper edge unstitched. Trim and clip the seams but do not turn right side out.

4. Slip the lining inside the stocking and align the upper raw edges. Baste ¼ inch from the edge.

5. Fold the ribbon or cord in half with raw edges even and pin in place on the inside of the stocking at the back seam; baste.

6. With right sides facing, stitch each green flannel strip to one long edge of a plaid flannel strip for the cuff and cuff facing. Press the seam open. Sew the short ends of each cuff strip together and press the seams open (Figure 1).

Figure 1
Prepare the cuff.

7. To make prairie points, fold each plaid square in half diagonally and press. Fold in half again and press (Figure 2).

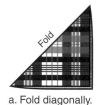

a. Fold diagonally. b. Fold in half again.

Figure 2
Making Prairie Points

8. With right sides together and raw edges even, arrange and pin the prairie points around the lower green edge of one cuff. Machine-baste ¼ inch from the raw edges.

9. With right sides facing, pin and stitch the cuff facing to the lower edge of the cuff with prairie points. Turn right side out and press. Stitch through all layers close to the lower edge of the green strip (Figure 3).

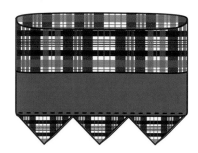

Figure 3
Edgestitch through all layers.

10. Tuck the cuff inside the stocking with the right side of the cuff against the wrong side of the stocking and with the side seam of cuff matching back seam of stocking. Align the raw edges, pin and stitch. Trim the seam to ¼ inch and zigzag the seam raw edges together. Turn the cuff to the right side of the stocking, covering the seam (Figure 4).

Figure 4
Sew cuff to inside of stocking;
turn down over right side.

11. Following the manufacturer's directions, cover three button forms with green flannel. Sew in place below the cuff, catching all layers of the front side of stocking.

Ornament

Materials
• ¼ yard red flannel for stocking body
• 5 x 8-inch piece green flannel for heel, toe and cuff
• Heavyweight black thread for decorative stitching
• 5 x 8-inch piece coordinating plaid flannel for upper cuff edge and prairie points
• 4½-inch-long piece ¼-inch-wide ribbon or cord for hanging loop
• 6-inch square lightweight paper-backed fusible web
• 2 (½-inch-diameter) buttons

Cutting
• Enlarge the pattern pieces on page 64 and trace onto pattern tracing paper or cloth and cut out.
• From the red flannel, cut two stockings.
• From the green flannel, cut one 1¼ x 7¼-inch strip for the cuff. Apply fusible web to the wrong side of the remaining flannel and fold in half with the fusible web inside. Pin the heel and toe pattern pieces in place on the folded flannel and cut out a pair of each.
• From the plaid flannel, cut one 1¾ x 7¼-inch strip for the cuff and one 1⅝ x 9¾-inch strip for prairie points. From the prairie-point strip, cut six 1⅝-inch squares for the prairie points.

Assembly
Note: Use ¼-inch-wide seam allowances unless otherwise directed.

1. Following the manufacturer's directions, fuse the heel and toe to each stocking. Stitch the inside edge of the heel and toe on each stocking using the topstitching needle and heavyweight thread and a blanket or appliqué stitch.

2. With right sides facing, stitch the stocking pieces together, leaving the upper edge open. Clip the curves as needed. Turn the stocking right side out.

3. Fold the ribbon or cord in half with raw edges even and pin in place on the inside of the stocking at the back seam; baste.

4. With right sides facing, sew the green strip to the plaid strip for the cuff. Press the seam open. With right sides facing and seam lines matching, sew the short ends of the cuff together. Turn under and press ¼ inch at the raw edge of the green strip.

5. Make six plaid prairie points as shown in Figure 2 on page 60 for the stocking. Machine-baste ¼ inch from the raw edges (Figure 5).

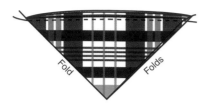

Figure 5
Machine-baste ¼" from raw edges.

6. Arrange the prairie points under the turned edge of the cuff with the cuff edge along the basting. Pin in place. Stitch close to the turned edge of the green strip.

7. Tuck the cuff inside the stocking with the right side of the cuff against the wrong side of the stocking. Stitch ¼ inch from the upper raw edge, and then zig-zag the seam allowance layers together. Turn the cuff to the outside over the seam allowance.

8. Sew two buttons in place below the prairie points on the front of the stocking.

Pillow

Materials
- ⅔ yard plaid flannel for pillow front and back, and prairie points
- 6 x 13-inch piece green flannel
- ½ yard red flannel for welting and covered buttons
- 2⅛ yards ¾-inch-diameter cotton cable cord for welting
- 12 x 16-inch ready-made pillow form
- 3 (1⅛-inch-diameter) covered-button forms
- Zipper foot

Cutting
- From the plaid flannel, cut one 12 x 13-inch rectangle for the pillow front, two 12 x 13-inch rectangles for the pillow back and four 4¼-inch squares for the prairie points.

- From the red flannel, cut enough 2¼-inch-wide true-bias strips to equal 80 inches when sewn together in one long strip using bias seams.

Assembly
Note: *Use ½-inch-wide seam allowances unless otherwise directed.*

1. Make a narrow double hem along one 13-inch-long edge of each plaid rectangle for the pillow back. Overlap the hemmed edges to create a 13 x 17-inch rectangle and baste the layers together (Figure 6).

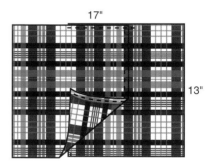

17"

13"

Figure 6
Overlap panels and baste edges together.

2. Fold the plaid squares as shown in Figure 2 on page 60 to make four prairie points.

3. Machine-baste ¼ inch from one long edge of the green strip. Arrange the prairie points with raw edges along the basting and tuck them into each other as shown in Figure 7. Machine-baste in place.

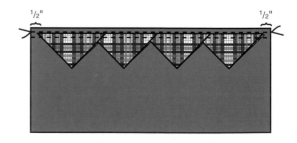

½"   ½"

Figure 7
Tuck prairie points into each other with raw edges along the basting. Baste in place.

4. Sew the red bias strips together with bias seams to make one long strip. Press the seams open.

5. Wrap the bias strip around the cord and stitch close to the cord with the zipper foot adjusted to the right of the needle (Figure 8).

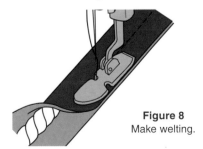

Figure 8
Make welting.

6. Cut a 13-inch-long piece from the completed welting. With raw edges aligned, pin and machine-baste the welting on top of the prairie

points on the green strip. With right sides facing, sew the green accent strip to the panel with the welting. Stitch from the green side so you can sew just inside the basting that holds the welting in place. Press the seam allowances toward the plaid (Figure 9).

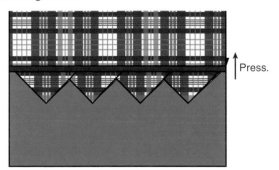

Figure 9
Sew plaid to green panel with prairie points and welting.

7. Following manufacturer's directions, cover three buttons with red flannel. Hand-sew in place on the pillow front, spacing evenly below the prairie points.

8. Machine-baste the welting to the outer edge of the pillow front, making a neat join along one long edge as shown in Figure 10. Clip the welting seam allowance as needed at the corners, rounding the welting around the corners.

9. With the pillow front on top, pin the pillow front and back together. Stitch just inside the basting that holds the welting in place. Turn the pillow cover right side out through the opening and tuck the pillow form inside.

Note: *A cozy flannel throw made from two layers of flannel (1¼ yards each of two colors of 44/45-inch-wide flannel) and bound in a contrasting color would make a great addition to this comfy group.* ✦

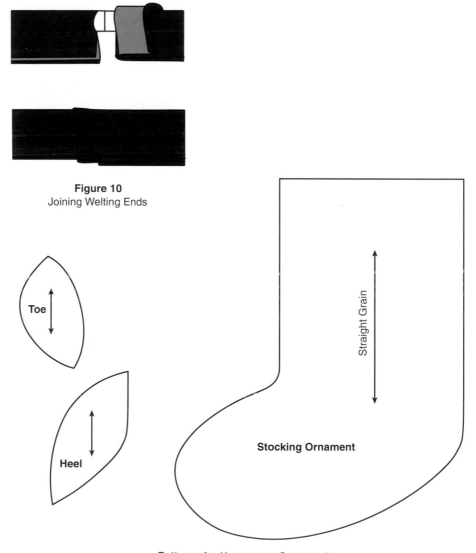

Figure 10
Joining Welting Ends

Toe

Heel

Straight Grain

Stocking Ornament

Patterns for Homespun Ornament
Enlarge 200%.

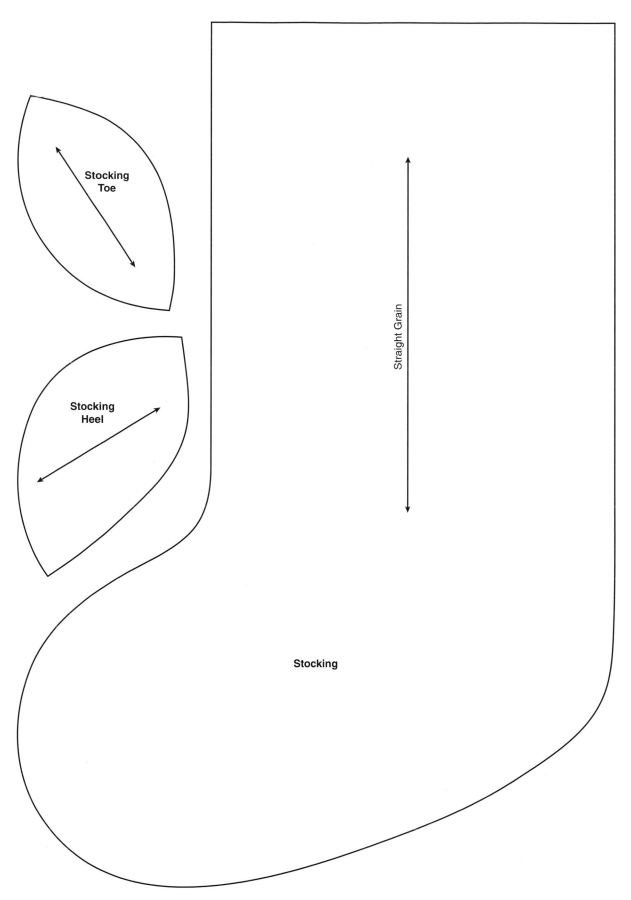

Stocking Toe

Stocking Heel

Straight Grain

Stocking

Patterns for Homespun Christmas Stocking
Enlarge 200%.

Christmas Sew-Phisticates

Designs by Pam Archer

Blend strips of assorted decorator chenille, embroidered silk and tapestry for a sophisticated take on Christmas decorating. Add sequins and beads for a sparkling and elegant approach to dressing up your home for the holidays with throw pillows and Christmas stockings.

Finished Sizes
Rectangular Pillow: 12 x 16 inches
Square Pillow: 12 inches square
Stocking: 8 x 21 inches

Materials for All Projects
• Size 10 sharp needle
• All-purpose thread to match fabric and beads
• Rotary cutter, mat and ruler
• Basic sewing tools and equipment

Rectangular Pillow

Materials
• 54-inch-wide decorator fabrics:
    ½ yard cranberry (diamond design)
    ½ yard burgundy jacquard chenille
    ½ yard light cranberry dobby weave
• ½ yard fusible knit interfacing
• ½ yard lightweight cotton batting
• 12 x 16-inch pillow form
• 7mm red sequins
• Red seed beads

Cutting
• From the cranberry (diamond design) fabric, cut one 5 x 13-inch and two 3 x 13-inch rectangles for the pillow front.
• From the jacquard chenille, cut two 3 x 13-inch and two 1½ x 13-inch rectangles for the pillow front.
• From the cranberry dobby weave fabric, cut two 2½ x 13-inch rectangles for the pillow front. Cut two 11 x 13-inch rectangles for the pillow back.

- From the fusible knit interfacing, cut a rectangle the same size as each of the fabric rectangles. Apply to the wrong side of each rectangle following the manufacturer's fusing directions.
- From the lightweight batting, cut one 13 x 17-inch and two 9½ x 13-inch rectangles.

Assembly

Note: Use ½-inch-wide seam allowances unless otherwise directed.

1. Position the 9½ x 13-inch pieces of batting on the wrong side of the 11 x 13-inch pillow backs and machine-baste a scant ½ inch from all raw edges with 1½ inches of cranberry fabric extending past one long edge on each piece (Figure 1).

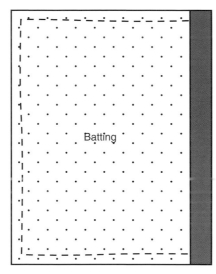

Figure 1
Machine-baste batting
to pillow back raw edges.

2. Trim the batting close to the basting to reduce bulk in the seams. Turn under and press ½ inch at the fabric extension. Turn the extension over the edge of the batting and press. Edgestitch in place through all the layers (Figure 2).

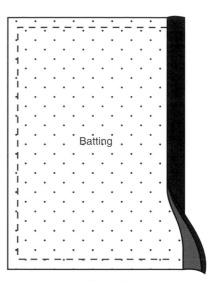

Figure 2
Wrap excess fabric over
batting edge. Stitch in place.

3. With both pillow backs faceup, arrange one pillow back over the other with the hemmed edges in the center to form a 13 x 17-inch rectangle. Pin the overlapping layers together and machine-baste ⅜ inch from the raw edges at the upper and lower edges (Figure 3).

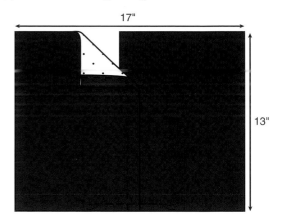

Figure 3
Baste pillow back panels together.

4. Arrange the pillow-top pieces as shown in Figure 4 and sew together using ½-inch-wide seams. Press all seams open and then trim each seam allowance to ¼ inch.

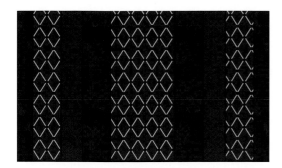

Figure 4
Sew strips together for pillow front.

5. Pin the 13 x 17-inch piece of batting to the wrong side of the pillow front. Machine-baste a scant ½ inch from the raw edges and trim the batting close to the basting. With right sides together, sew the pillow front and back together around the outer edges.

Note: *To turn really smooth corners, adjust the seam line as shown in Figure 5. Although it looks wrong, it actually prevents corners that are not square or that appear overly pointed.*

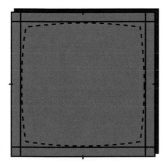

Figure 5
Stitch slightly bowed corners
for smoother turned corners.

6. Turn the pillow cover right side out through the back opening.

7. Add a sequin with a seed bead on top to each diamond point. Using a needle with a doubled thread, bring the needle up through the center of each point. Place one sequin and one seed bead on the needle and slide into place. Thread the needle back through the sequin's hole but not the

bead's hole and return the needle to the wrong side (Figure 6). Pull the thread taut and secure the sequin and bead. Repeat to bead the remaining diamond points.

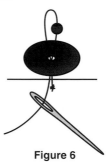

Figure 6
Sew sequins and seed beads
at diamond intersections.

8. Insert the pillow form through the back opening.

Square Pillow

Materials
- ½ yard green embroidered silk for pillow front and back
- 6 x 15-inch scrap green solid fabric for pillow front
- 6 x 15-inch scrap green brocade for pillow front
- ½ yard 1½-inch-wide gold-edged sheer ribbon
- ½ yard fusible knit interfacing
- ½ yard lightweight cotton batting
- 12-inch-square pillow form
- 4mm green sequins
- Gold seed beads

Cutting

- From the green solid, cut one 4 x 13-inch rectangle for the pillow front.
- From the green embroidered silk, cut two 8½ x 13-inch rectangles for the pillow back. Cut two 3 x 13-inch and two 2½ x 13-inch strips for the pillow front.
- From the green brocade, cut two 2 x 13-inch rectangles.
- From the fusible knit interfacing, cut rectangles to match the fabric rectangles. Apply to the wrong side of each rectangle following the manufacturer's fusing directions.
- From the lightweight batting, cut one 13-inch square and two 7 x 13-inch rectangles.
- Cut one 13½-inch piece of ribbon.

Assembly

Note: Use ½-inch-wide seam allowances unless otherwise directed.

1. Position the 7 x 13-inch pieces of batting on the wrong side of the 8½ x 13-inch pillow backs, and machine-baste a scant ½ inch from all raw edges with 1½ inches of the green embroidered fabric extending past one long edge on each piece as shown in Figure 1 on page 68 for the rectangular pillow. Trim the batting close to the basting to reduce bulk in the seams.

2. Turn under and press ½ inch from the fabric extension. Turn the extension over the edge of the batting and press. Edgestitch in place through all the layers as shown in Figure 2 on page 68 for the rectangular pillow.

3. With both pillow backs face up, arrange one pillow back over the other with the hemmed edges in the center forming a 13-inch square. Pin the overlapping layers together and machine-baste ⅜ inch from the raw edges at upper and lower edges as shown in Figure 3 on page 68 for the rectangular pillow.

4. With right sides up, center the ribbon on the 4½ x 13-inch green solid rectangle. Pin in place, and with matching thread, stitch along both long edges of the ribbon.

5. Arrange the pieces for the pillow top as shown in Figure 7 and sew together with ½-inch-wide seams. Press the seams open and trim all seam allowances to ¼ inch.

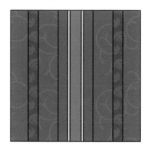

Figure 7
Sew strips together for pillow front.

6. Pin the 13-inch square of batting to the wrong side of the completed pillow front. Machine-baste a scant ½ inch from the raw edges and trim the batting close to the basting.

7. With right sides together, sew the pillow front and back together around the outer edges. Refer to the Note and Figure 5 on page 69 for the rectangular pillow. Turn the pillow cover right side out through the back opening.

8. Following the embroidered design, add bead/sequin embellishments as directed in step 7 for the rectangular pillow on page 69.

9. Insert the pillow form through the back opening.

Stocking

Materials for One Stocking
- ¾ yard green embroidered silk for stocking
- ¾ yard green solid for lining
- 14 x 18-inch scrap green solid for cuff
- 6 x 15-inch scrap gold-and-green jacquard satin for cuff
- ¾ yard fusible knit interfacing
- ½ yard 1½-inch-wide gold-edged sheer ribbon
- ⅓ yard ½-inch-wide green velvet ribbon
- ¾ yard lightweight cotton batting
- 4mm green sequins
- Gold seed beads
- Pinking shears
- Pattern tracing paper or cloth

Cutting
- Enlarge the stocking pattern (Figure 8 on page 72) onto pattern tracing paper or cloth and cut out.
- Use the pattern to cut two stockings each from the green embroidered silk, lining fabric, fusible interfacing and cotton batting. From the remaining embroidered silk, cut two 1¾ x 17-inch rectangles.
- From the gold-and-green jacquard, cut two 2 x 17-inch rectangles for the cuff.
- From the green solid, cut one 2½ x 17-inch rectangle and one 6 x 17-inch rectangle for the cuff lining.
- From the remaining fusible knit interfacing, cut rectangles to match the fabric rectangles. Apply to the wrong side of each rectangle following the manufacturer's fusing directions.
- Cut one 17-inch length of 1½-inch-wide gold-edged ribbon and one 10-inch length of green velvet ribbon.

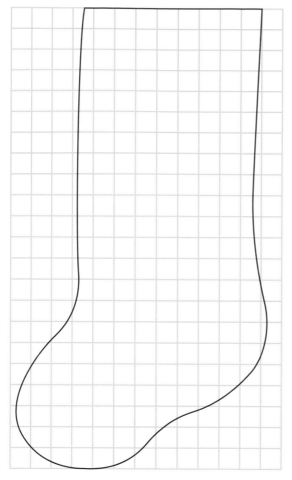

Figure 8
Pattern for Christmas Sew-Phisticate Stocking
1 square = 1"

Assembly

Note: *Use ½-inch-wide seam allowances.*

1. Baste a batting stocking to the wrong side of each silk stocking piece. Trim close to the basting to reduce bulk.

2. With right sides facing, pin and stitch the silk/batting stockings together; leave the upper edge

unstitched. Trim the seam allowance to ¼ inch, using pinking shears to automatically notch out fullness in the curves of the toe. Turn the stocking right side out and press. Repeat with the lining pieces, but leave a 5-inch-long opening in the back seam for turning. Do not turn the lining right side out.

3. Arrange the strips for the cuff as shown in Figure 9 and sew together with ½-inch-wide seam allowances. Press the seams open and trim the seam allowances to ¼ inch.

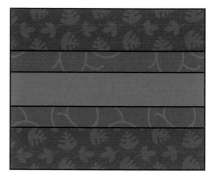

Figure 9
Sew strips together for cuff.

4. Center the gold-edged ribbon on the right side of the 2½-inch-wide strip of green solid fabric. Pin in place and then stitch along both long edges using matching thread in the needle.

5. Fold the pieced strip in half with short raw edges even and right sides facing. Stitch ½ inch from the raw edges and press the seam open. Repeat with the 6 x 17-inch lining strip. Trim the seam allowances in the lining to ¼ inch and the seam in the cuff to ⅜ inch.

6. With the seams and raw edges aligned and right sides facing, pin and stitch the cuff to the cuff lining along one long edge. Trim the seam to ¼ inch (Figure 10).

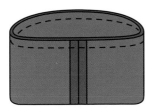

Figure 10
Sew cuff to cuff lining.

7. Turn the cuff right side out and press. Machine-baste the upper raw edges together.

8. Slip the cuff over the stocking and align all raw edges. Machine-baste in place.

9. Fold the velvet ribbon in half, right side out, to form a hanging loop. Align the raw ends at the back seam line on the right side of the stocking and baste in place (Figure 11).

Figure 11
Baste cuff and hanging
loop to stocking upper edge.

10. Tuck the stocking into the lining with right sides facing and upper raw edges aligned. Stitch ½ inch from the upper edges. Turn the stocking right side out through the opening in the side of the lining.

11. Turn under and press the opening edges in the lining and edgestitch the layers together.

12. Tuck the lining inside the stocking and stitch in the ditch of the first seam in the cuff, stitching through all layers to anchor the cuff.

13. Add sequins and beads as desired following the directions in step 7 for the rectangular pillow on page 69. ✦

Beaded Sequins

An easy way to add a festive feel to any project is with the simple pairing of sequins and seed beads. Their reflective qualities say "I'm special" while adding texture and visual interest.

• **For a successful beading project,** start small. Look to your patterned fabric for inspiration. It provides a built-in road map for bead placement. While the project is sewn but still flat, play with bead and sequin colors, sizes and placements to achieve a pleasing placement and design.

• **Seed beads come in a variety of sizes.** Opt for size 7–10 since they are easier to sew in place. Check to make sure that a double-threaded needle will pass through the seed bead easily. While beading thread such as Nymo can be used for this project, consider using a polyester sewing thread that has been doubled and waxed to eliminate fraying from sewing friction.

• **When selecting sequins,** think about the amount of surface and the fabric to be covered; larger, denser designs can handle larger sequins while lighter, more delicate design lines will fare better with a smaller, more proportionate sequin. Pair it with a bead in a matching or coordinating color picked up from the fabric for great visual interest and holiday sparkle.

The Gifted Mantel

Design by Marta Alto

No need for Christmas stockings with this elegant mantel cover. Before Christmas, use the pockets as holders for your favorite greeting cards from friends and family. Then remove them on Christmas Eve so Santa can tuck gifts and trinkets in them to greet the family on Christmas morn.

Finished Size

9 x 9 x 72 inches, excluding fringe trim and optional end drops, to fit a 10 x 72-inch mantel. Adjust cutting dimensions to fit your mantel.

Materials

- 2¼ yards 44/45-inch-wide silk dupioni
- 1⅛ yards cotton in matching color for lining
- 9 x 74-inch piece cotton batting for front drop
- 11 x 74-inch strip cotton batting for mantel cover
- 5½ x 74-inch strip cotton batting for pocket panel
- 2 (9 x 11-inch) strips cotton batting for optional end drops
- 4 yards tassel trim with decorative header
- 4¼ yards coordinating twisted-cord welting
- All-purpose thread to match fabric and trims
- Gold metallic embroidery thread
- Sewing machine needle for metalic thread
- Clear monofilament thread
- Temporary spray adhesive
- Chalk marker
- Zipper foot
- Basic sewing tools and equipment

Cutting

- From the length of the silk dupioni, cut two 9 x 73-inch strips for the front drop and lining, one 11 x 73-inch strip for the mantel cover and one 5½ x 73-inch-wide strip for the pocket panel.
- Optional: For end drops, cut four 9 x 11-inch panels from silk dupioni.
- From the lining fabric, cut two 11 x 37-inch panels and two 5½ x 37-inch panels. Sew each pair of panels together along short ends using a ¼-inch-wide seam; press the seam open.

Assembly

Note: *Use ½-inch-wide seam allowances unless otherwise directed.*

1. Apply a light coat of temporary spray adhesive to the wrong side of the 5½-inch-wide silk pocket panel and smooth in place on the batting strip. Alternatively, pin the layers together.

2. Pin the twisted-cord welting to one long edge of the pocket panel with the seam-allowance edge

aligned with the raw edges. Use the zipper foot to stitch close to the cord (Figure 1).

Figure 1
Sew twisted-cord welting to pocket panel.

3. With right sides facing, sew the pocket lining panel to the pocket panel along the upper edge. Turn the lining to the back of the panel and press as needed. Trim so the finished panel measures 73 inches long. Set aside.

4. Apply a light coat of temporary spray adhesive to the wrong side of the 9-inch-wide silk panel for the front drop. Smooth in place on the batting strip for the drop. Apply the silk lining panel to the remaining side of the batting in the same manner.

5. Change to the metallic sewing machine needle and thread with metallic thread. Use a chalk marker to mark a diagonal grid of diamonds spaced 1 inch apart on the silk. For best results, mark one direction and stitch through all layers. Then, draw the grid lines in the opposite direction and stitch (Figure 2).

Figure 2
Draw and quilt on diagonal grid.

6. Sew twisted-cord welting to one long edge of the quilted drop panel. Trim the panel as needed to measure 73 inches long.

7. Pin the pocket panel to the front drop panel with bottom raw edges matching. Machine-baste ⅜ inch from the side and bottom edges.

8. Divide the pocket panel into the desired number of pockets and chalk-mark the stitching lines. Pin along the chalk lines with the pin points toward the bottom edge.

Note: *The number of pockets and width will depend on the finished length of the mantel cover for your fireplace.*

Machine-stitch along the pocket lines with metallic thread in the needle. Stitch from the bottom edge up to the welting, backstitching at the beginning and end of the stitching and removing pins as you reach them (Figure 3).

Front drop   Pocket panel

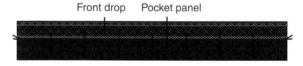

Figure 3
Mark, pin and stitch pocket sections through all layers.

9. With right sides facing, pin and sew the lining strip and the mantel cover together along one long edge. Use a ¼-inch-wide seam. If you are not adding end drops, sew along the two short ends as well. Turn right side out and press.

10. With silk sides facing, pin the mantel cover to the upper piped edge of the front drop panel. Stitch through all layers just inside the first stitching line that holds the welting in place (Figure 4).

Figure 4
Sew mantel cover to front drop/pocket panel.

11. Place the silk lining strip for the front drop facedown on the right side of the mantel cover lining. Stitch through all layers on top of previous stitching. Turn the lining down over the seam allowance and against the back of the front drop/pocket panel.

12. Press the lining toward the drop. Pin all layers together along the raw edges. Serge- or zigzag-finish the raw edges together, removing the pins as you reach them. Use a wide stitch to help compact the layers together (Figure 5).

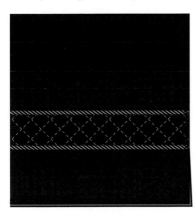

Figure 5
Serge all raw edges together
along side and bottom.

13. Prepare and add end drops if desired (see End Drops).

14. Pin the tassel trim in place over the serged edges and zigzag in place using a zigzag setting of 3.5mm wide x 2.5mm long. Use monofilament thread in the needle for invisible stitching. ✦

End Drops

1. Apply spray adhesive to the wrong side of two silk rectangles and smooth each one in place on a batting rectangle. Mark a diagonal grid and stitch to quilt the layers together as directed in step 5 for the front drop.

2. Pin the lining to one short end of each rectangle and stitch ¼ inch from the raw edges. Turn right side out and press. Serge- or zigzag-finish the remaining raw edges, sewing all layers together (Figure 1).

Figure 1
Serge raw edges together
at sides and bottom.

3. Lap the finished end of the drop over the serged end of the mantel cover and topstitch in place (Figure 2).

Figure 2
Lap end drop over short
end of mantel cover and stitch.

'Tis the Season

Designs By Carol Zentgraf

'Tis the season to pull out all the stops and deck the house to the nines. For this fun ensemble, choose a set of four coordinating decorator fabrics and then stitch up this set featuring mantel cover, tree skirt and stocking.

Finished Sizes
Mantel Cover: 9 x 54 inches with 9-inch-long pennants
Stocking: 11 x 22 inches
Tree Skirt: 54 inches in diameter

Mantel Cover

Materials
- 54-inch-wide coordinating decorator fabrics
    - 1⅝ yards floral pattern
    - 1⅝ yards dot pattern
    - ⅔ yard coordinating stripe
- ⅔ yard 54-inch-wide silk dupioni
- Pattern tracing cloth or paper
- 3⅔ yards twisted-cord welting
- 8 (¾-inch-diameter) covered-button forms
- 8 (6-inch-long) decorator tassels
- Permanent fabric adhesive
- Basic sewing tools and equipment

Cutting
- Enlarge the pennant pattern (Figure 1 on page 80) and trace onto pattern tracing cloth or paper.
- From the floral fabric, cut one 10 x 55-inch rectangle for the mantel-cover base and two pennants for the ends. Repeat with the dot fabric.
- For the front, cut six pennants each from the floral, stripe and dupioni fabrics—a total of 18 pieces.

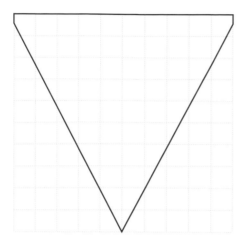

Figure 1
'Tis the Season Mantel Pennant
1 square = 1"

Assembly

Note: *Use ½-inch-wide seam allowances.*

1. To make each end pennant, pin a floral pennant to a dot pennant. Sew the side edges together, leaving the upper edge open. Rather than making a sharp pivot at the point, stop shy of the point so you can stitch two stitches across the point (Figure 2). Clip across the point to eliminate bulk. Turn right side out and press. Machine-baste the upper edges together.

Figure 2
Take 2 stitches across the point.

2. To make each front pennant, sew two matching pennants together along the side edges, pivoting as directed above. Trim the point, turn right side out and press. Baste the upper edges together.

3. Mark the center at the upper edge of each silk dupioni pennant. Pin a stripe and a floral

pennant on top of each dupioni pennant, with edges meeting at the center mark and the upper edges aligned. Baste the upper edges together (Figure 3).

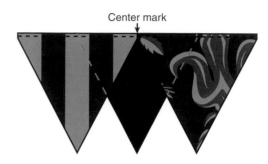

Figure 3
Lap and baste pennants in sets of 3.

4. Beginning and ending in the center of the back edge, baste the twisted-cord welting to the long floral rectangle with the welting lip and fabric edges even.

5. Baste an end pennant to each end of the floral rectangle with raw edges even and floral sides together (Figure 4).

Figure 4
Sew a pennant to each short end
of the cord-trimmed mantel strip.

6. With raw edges even and the dupioni pennants on top, center and pin the three sets of three pennants to the right side of the floral rectangle (Figure 5).

Figure 5
Baste pennant sets to front
edge over corded welting.

7. With all pennants sandwiched between the layers, sew the long dot rectangle to the floral rectangle, leaving an opening along the back edge for turning. Turn right side out and press. Slipstitch the opening closed.

8. Cover the buttons with fabric scraps following the package directions. Sew a button to each floral and stripe pennant, positioning them 1 inch from the points.

9. Hang a tassel on each button, wrapping the loop around the button as many times as possible. Secure the loops behind the buttons with fabric adhesive.

Stocking

Materials for One Stocking
- 54-inch-wide decorator fabrics
  - ⅝ yard stripe for stocking
  - ⅝ yard coordinating solid for lining
- ⅓ yard 54-inch-wide silk dupioni for pennant flap
- Scraps coordinating fabric for heel and toe
- Pattern tracing cloth or paper
- Chalk or chalk pencil
- ⅔ yard coordinating tassel trim for upper edge
- ⅔ yard each of 2 decorative gimp trims
- 1 (¾-inch-diameter) covered-button form
- 6-inch-long piece ¾-inch-wide coordinating ribbon for loop hanger
- 2 (6-inch long) tassels in coordinating colors
- Lightweight paper-backed fusible web
- Permanent fabric adhesive
- Basic sewing tools and equipment

Cutting & Preparation
- Enlarge the stocking, pennant flap, toe and heel patterns on page 85 and trace onto pattern tracing cloth or paper.
- Cut two stockings each, reversing one of each, from the stripe and from the lining fabric.
- Cut two pennant flaps from the silk dupioni.
- Trace the heel and toe patterns onto the paper side of the fusible web and cut out with a ¼-inch margin all around. Following the manufacturer's directions, fuse the heel and toe to the wrong side of the fabric scraps. Cut out on the drawn lines.

Assembly

Note: *Use ½-inch-wide seam allowances.*

1. Remove the paper backing from the heel and toe pieces. Fuse to one stocking piece, following the manufacturer's directions.

2. Position and glue or sew a piece of each gimp trim around the toe and heel.

3. On the wrong side of one of the pennant flaps, mark the seam-line intersection at the corners with chalk or chalk pencil as shown in Figure 1. With right sides facing, sew the flap pieces together, beginning and ending at the intersections with backstitching.

Figure 1
Sew pennant flaps together.

4. Trim the point to remove bulk and turn right side out. Press. Baste the flap to the stocking front, aligning upper edges. (Figure 2)

Figure 2
Baste flap to front of stocking at upper edge.

5. Sew the stocking front to the back, leaving the upper edges unstitched. Turn right side out and press the edges. Fold the ribbon in half to make a loop. With the loop ends even with the upper edge of the stocking, baste the loop ends to the right side of the stocking back (Figure 3).

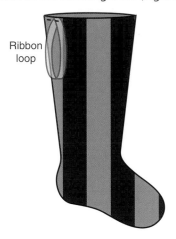

Figure 3
Baste loop ends to upper edge of stocking back.

6. Sew the lining front and back together, using a ⅝-inch-wide seam allowance so the lining will fit smoothly inside the stocking. Leave a 4-inch opening in the back seam (Figure 4).

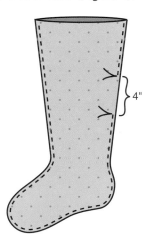

Figure 4
Sew lining pieces together.

7. With right sides facing, tuck the stocking into the lining. Align the seam lines and upper edges and stitch together around the upper edge. Turn the stocking right side out through the opening in

the lining. Turn in the opening edges in the lining and edgestitch together. Tuck the lining inside the stocking and press.

8. Position tassel trim at the upper edge and sew in place, making a neat join on the back of the stocking close to the back seam.

9. Cover the button with a scrap of the desired fabric following the package directions. Position the button 1 inch above the flap point and sew in place.

10. Wrap the loops of the two tassels around the button as many times as possible; secure behind the button with fabric adhesive.

Tree Skirt

Materials
- ¾ yard each 4 coordinating 54-inch-wide decorator fabrics
- 2 yards 54-inch-wide solid-color decorator fabric for lining
- 6½ yards tassel trim
- 3½ yards twisted-cord welting
- 1 yard ¾-inch-wide coordinating ribbon
- Pattern tracing cloth or paper
- Permanent fabric adhesive
- Masking tape
- Zipper foot
- Basic sewing tools and equipment

Cutting & Planning

- Enlarge the tree skirt panel pattern (Figure 1) and trace onto pattern tracing cloth or paper and cut out.

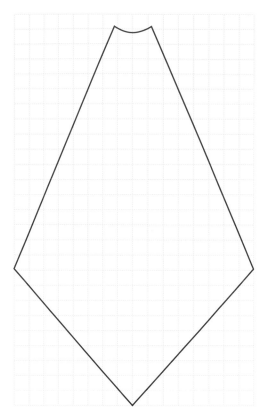

Figure 1
'Tis the Season Tree Skirt Panel
1 square = 1"

- Use the pattern to cut two panels from each of the four decorator fabrics and eight panels from the solid-color fabric for the lining.

Assembly

Note: *Use ½-inch-wide seam allowances.*

1. Cut twisted-cord welting into seven equal lengths. Apply fabric adhesive to the cut ends to prevent the cords from untwisting or wrap with a narrow strip of masking tape.

2. Arrange the skirt panels in the desired order and baste the welting to the right side along the right-hand edge of each of seven adjacent panels (Figure 2), leaving two adjacent edges free of welting. Sew the panels together, leaving the two adjacent untrimmed edges unstitched for the skirt opening as shown in Figure 3.

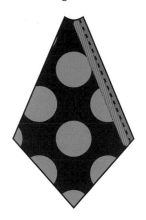

Figure 2
Machine-baste twisted cord welting
to right-hand edge of 7 panels.

Unstitched

Figure 3
Arrange the panels. Sew together.

3. To make the lining, sew the solid-color panels together, leaving one seam unstitched as for the skirt.

4. Cut the ribbon in half. Baste the ribbon ends to the upper open edges of the lining as shown in Figure 4.

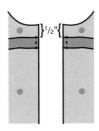

Figure 4
Baste ribbon to upper edges at opening.

5. Pin the tree skirt to the lining with all edges even and the ribbon ties sandwiched between the layers. Sew the edges together, leaving a 12-inch-long section unstitched in the center of one of the opening edges for turning. Clip the curves and corners, and trim excess cord from the seam allowance. Turn right side out and press, turning the opening edges in. Stitch the edges together.

6. Pin and sew tassel trim along the upper and lower edges of the skirt right side. ✦

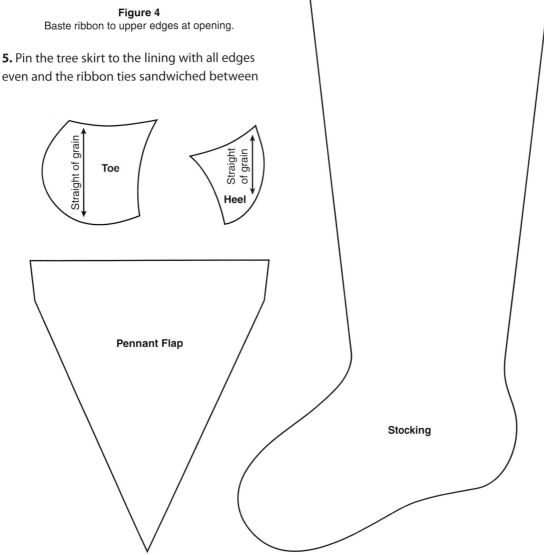

Pattern Pieces for 'Tis the Season Stocking
Enlarge 400%.

Angelina Poinsettias

Designs by Lynn Weglarz

Combine Angelina hot-fix fibers with decorative stitching to create beautiful poinsettia ornaments and a matching stocking to hang by the chimney with care.

Finished Sizes
Poinsettia Stocking: 11½ x 18 inches
Poinsettia Ornament: 8¼ x 5 inches

Poinsettia Stocking

Materials
- ½ yard white-on-white cotton jacquard for stocking
- ¼ yard contrasting cotton print for the cuff
- ½ yard white-on-white cotton for lining
- ¾ yard ¼- or ⅜-inch-diameter twisted-cord piping
- ¼ yard ¼-inch-wide ribbon for hanger
- Angelina hot-fix Fibers
    - 1 package Raspberry
    - 1 package Gold Angelina
    - 1 package Violette Crystalina
    - 1 package of Peacock
- 2 (7-inch) squares water-soluble stabilizer
- 8-inch square lightweight fusible web
- All-purpose thread to match stocking fabric
- ½ yard lightweight batting
- Gold and dark green metallic embroidery thread
- 9 clear yellow beads for poinsettia center
- Sewing machine needle for metallic thread
- Temporary spray adhesive
- 2 Teflon release cloths or 2 sheets parchment paper
- Pattern tracing paper or cloth
- Chalk marker
- Template plastic
- Basic sewing tools and equipment

Cutting
- Enlarge the stocking and cuff pattern pieces as directed on pages 91 and 92 onto pattern tracing paper or cloth. Cut out.
- Cut two stockings each from the jacquard, lining and lightweight batting. Make sure to cut a stocking front and back from each fabric.
- From the print for the cuff, cut two cuffs on the fold; cut one on the fold from the batting.

Assembly
Note: Use ½-inch-wide seam allowances unless otherwise directed. Before you begin, read Success with Angelina on page 90.

1. Apply a light coat of temporary spray adhesive to one side of each piece of batting and smooth a stocking piece faceup on top.

2. Lay an 8-inch square of fusible web on one of the Teflon release cloths (or a piece of parchment paper). Arrange Violette Crystalina Angelina fibers on top of the fusible web. Drizzle Peacock Angelina fibers on top and then place the second Teflon release cloth on top of the fibers. Press following package directions and then peel the fused fibers from the Teflon release cloth.

3. Trace the poinsettia leaf templates on page 93 onto the template plastic and cut out.

4. Trace around the templates on the right side of the fused fibers (fusible web is wrong side). You will need three large leaves and two small leaves. Cut out each shape. Position the leaves on the stocking front about 12 inches below the upper edge and fuse in place.

5. Draw the veins on each leaf with a chalk marker, and then stitch using the green metallic thread and the needle for metallic thread in the machine (Figure 1).

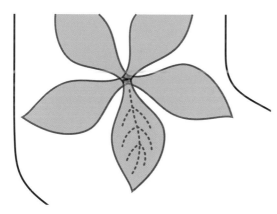

Figure 1
Stitch veins in each leaf.

6. Place one square of water-soluble stabilizer over the poinsettia shape on page 93 and trace. On the remaining square of stabilizer, add a layer of Raspberry Angelina fibers and then drizzle with Gold Angelina. Place the water-soluble stabilizer on top to make a "sandwich." Pin the layers together.

7. Adjust the sewing machine for a narrow satin stitch and stitch over the traced lines using gold metallic thread and needle for metallic thread on the machine. As you reach the points, gradually decrease the stitch width; after turning the point, gradually increase the stitch width. After completing all stitching, carefully pull away the stabilizer and rinse if necessary to remove any stubborn bits. Trim the excess Angelina fiber close to the stitching without snipping the stitches. Position the poinsettia over the leaves on the stocking front and pin in place. Hand-sew nine yellow beads to the center through all layers.

8. With right sides facing, stitch the stocking pieces together; leaving the upper edges unstitched; repeat for the stocking lining pieces. For a good fit, use a ½-inch-wide seam allowance on the stocking and a ⅝-inch-wide seam allowance on the lining so it fits smoothly inside. Trim the seams to ¼ inch and clip the curves. Turn the stocking right side out, but leave the lining wrong side out.

9. Wrong sides together, slip the lining into the stocking and align the upper raw edges. Machine-baste the layers together.

10. Apply a light coat of spray adhesive to one side of the cuff batting and smooth one cuff in place right side up. Position the twisted-cord piping around the curved edge and machine-baste in place. Clip the seam allowance edge of the trim as needed for a smooth fit.

11. With right sides facing and the piped cuff facing you, pin and stitch the cuff layers together just inside the first row of piping stitching. Clip the seam and turn right side out. Fold in half and mark the fold with a small clip at the upper raw edges.

12. Fold the ribbon for the hanger in half and align the raw edges with the upper edge on the inside of the stocking at the back seam; baste in place.

13. Turn the stocking lining side out. Pin the cuff to the stocking upper edge with the center of the cuff matching the front seam of the stocking and the cuff ends overlapping at the back seam. Pin the cuff to the upper edge with a 1-inch overlap. Stitch the seam and then zigzag the seam allowance edges together (Figure 2).

Figure 2
Stitch cuff to stocking.

14. Turn the stocking right side out and turn the cuff down over the seam.

Poinsettia Ornaments

Materials for Three Ornaments

- Angelina hot-fix Fibers
    - 1 package Raspberry
    - 1 package Gold
    - 1 package Violette Crystalina
    - 1 package Peacock
- 19½ x 36-inch piece water-soluble stabilizer
- ⅓ yard lightweight fusible web
- ⅝ yard ⅛- or ¼-inch-wide ribbon
- Gold metallic thread
- 27 clear yellow beads for poinsettia centers
- Sewing machine needle for metallic thread
- 2 Teflon release cloths or sheets of parchment paper
- Craft or fabric glue
- Chalk marker
- Template plastic
- Basic sewing tools and equipment

Assembly

1. For each ornament, trace the poinsettia shape onto water-soluble stabilizer two times. Referring to steps 4 and 5 for the stocking, create two poinsettias for each ornament.

2. Cut three 8-inch squares of fusible web. Lay an 8-inch square of fusible web on one of the Teflon release cloths (or a piece of parchment paper). Arrange Violette Crystalina Angelina fibers on top of the fusible web. Drizzle Peacock Angelina fibers on top and then place the second Teflon release cloth on top of the fibers. Press following package directions and then peel the fused fibers from the Teflon release cloth.

3. Trace the poinsettia leaf templates on page 91 onto the template plastic and cut out. Trace around the templates on the right side of the fused fibers (fusible web is wrong side), tracing one set of two for each ornament. Flip the templates and trace one reverse set for each ornament. Cut out.

Success With Angelina

Angelina fibers are made to fuse together at a low temperature setting, about 225 degrees or the silk setting on your iron. For best results:

• **Do not use steam.** If your iron is too hot, the fibers will discolor and you will see steam-hole vent impressions. Try using a soleplate on the bottom of your iron to eliminate the problem of making steam vent impressions.

• **Make a small sample** to test the temperature setting on your iron. The fibers typically do not adhere to anything but themselves, but do use either a Teflon release cloth or parchment paper (which can be found in the grocery store, usually in the baking aisle.) Lay the Teflon release cloth or parchment paper on the ironing board, put the Angelina Fibers on top making sure the fibers are of even thickness and slightly dense, and then add the remaining release cloth. Press gently.

• **Gently remove the cloths** and the fused fiber fabric is ready to cut into the desired shapes. Try color variations by blending the fibers together, or lay colors one on top of the other. Or use a higher heat setting on the iron, because sometimes the discoloring that happens is the right color.

4. Arrange the leaves in matching sets, fusible side to fusible side. Cover with the Teflon release cloth and fuse to create three pairs of double-sided Angelina leaves. Using a chalk marker, draw the vein lines onto the leaves. Stitch the veins using green metallic thread and needle for metallic thread on the machine.

5. To assemble an ornament, lay one of the poinsettia shapes right side down and position a pair of leaves on top. Add another poinsettia right side up. Sew nine beads to the center on each side of each poinsettia, making sure to catch the leaves in place.

6. For each ornament, cut an 8-inch-long piece of ribbon. Bring the raw ends together and tack. Tuck the tacked ends between the flower layers and glue in place. ✦

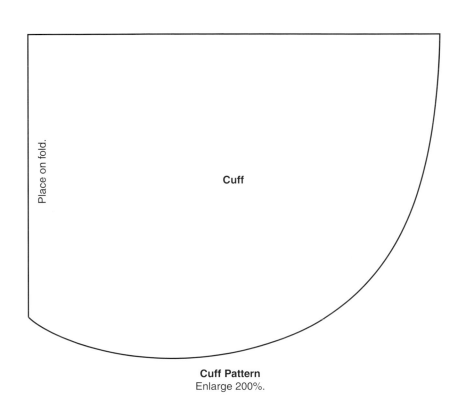

Place on fold.

Cuff

Cuff Pattern
Enlarge 200%.

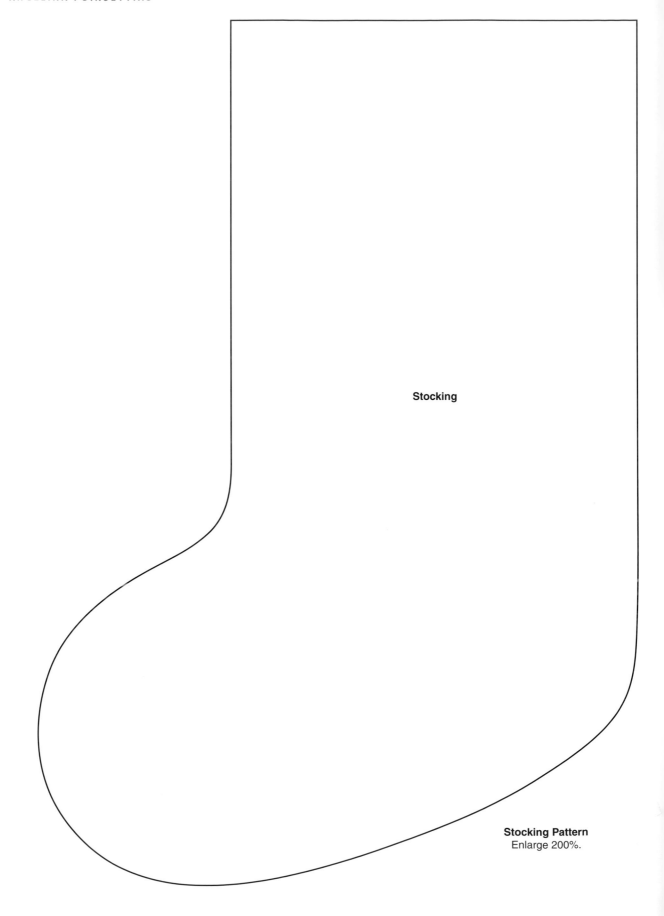

Stocking

Stocking Pattern
Enlarge 200%.

Large

Small

Patterns for Angelina Poinsettias & Leaves
Actual size.

Partridge on a Pillow

Design by Janis Bullis

This pretty partridge has forsaken its traditional pear tree to roost on an elegant pillow for your holiday decor. Satin-stitching enhances the edges of the fused raw-edge appliqués.

Finished Size
16 inches square, excluding fringe

Materials
- ½ yard gold cotton damask
- 10 x 14-inch piece green cotton damask
- 10 x 14-inch piece red cotton damask
- 6 x 10-inch piece purple cotton damask
- 2 yards 1½-inch-wide brush fringe trim
- Template plastic
- ⅜ yard 18-inch-wide paper-backed lightweight fusible web
- Rayon embroidery thread to match damask colors
- 16-inch-square pillow form
- Basic sewing tools and equipment

Cutting
- From the gold damask, cut two 17-inch squares for the pillow front and back, and one 6 x 10-inch rectangle for the wing appliqué.

- Enlarge the appliqué pieces as directed on page 97 and trace onto template plastic. Cut out carefully. Reverse each template on the paper side of the fusible web with ½ inch of space between shapes. Trace around each one. Cut out each piece with a ¼-inch-wide allowance all around. Remove the backing paper.

Assembly
Note: *Use a ½-inch-wide seam allowance.*

1. Following the manufacturer's directions, apply each piece of fusible web to the wrong side of a fabric rectangle of the appropriate color for each appliqué piece. Cut out each appliqué along the traced lines and remove the paper backing.

2. Referring to the appliqué design on page 97, arrange the pieces on the right side of one

of the 17-inch gold damask squares. Fuse in place following the manufacturer's directions.

3. Read through the directions for Satin-Stitch Appliqué below. Changing thread color for each piece, satin-stitch over the raw edges of each appliqué; draw the needle threads to the underside and tie off securely with the bobbin threads where stitching ends for each color.

4. On the right side of the appliquéd pillow front, pin and machine-baste the fringe in place with the trim header edge even with the cut edge and rounding it around the corners. With right sides facing, pin the pillow back to the pillow front along all edges. Stitch, leaving a 10-inch-long opening in the center of the bottom edge for turning (Figure 1).

10" opening

Figure 1
Sew front to back.

5. Turn the pillow cover right side out through the opening and insert the pillow form. Turn in the opening edges and slipstitch them together. ✦

Satin-Stitch Appliqué

Adjust your machine and test the satin-stitching settings on scraps as directed below.

1. Attach the zigzag, decorative or satin-stitch presser foot. Adjust the machine for a medium-width satin stitch.

2. Loosen the upper thread tension slightly so the bobbin tension will pull the top thread to the underside.

3. Using small scraps of fabric, fuse an appliqué sample to a base fabric sample to mimic the actual appliqué. Test the stitch width and length on the sample before stitching on the actual appliqué. Adjust as needed to suit your fabric for the best edge coverage.

4. Guide the fabric to allow the right-hand swing of the needle to jump over the appliqué edge into the fabric behind it. The left-hand swing should penetrate the appliqué. Turn the assembly slowly and smoothly on curves to guide the appliqué edge so that it is always held at a 90-degree angle to the stitch width.

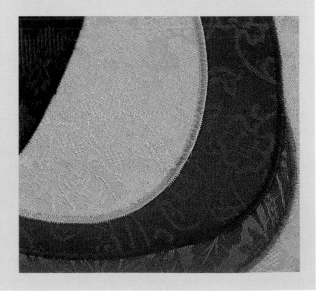

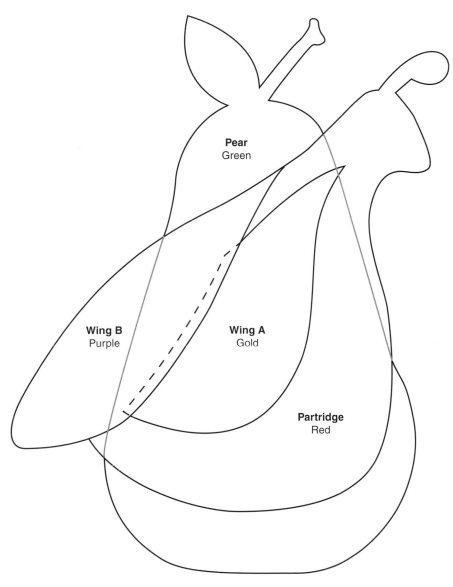

Pear
Green

Wing B
Purple

Wing A
Gold

Partridge
Red

Partridge on a Pillow
Templates and Placement Guide
Enlarge 200%.

The Birds' Christmas

Designs by Marta Alto

Snowy white satin is the perfect backdrop for finely detailed birds surrounded by holiday greens. Use the tasseled diamond ornaments as tree decor or gifts for guests at a holiday tea with a winter nature theme. Hang them at your mantel or tuck them into the greens of a woodland wreath. Gold lamé piping is the perfect edging.

Finished Size
5½ x 8 inches, excluding hanger and tassels

Materials for Four Ornaments
- ½ yard white polyester crepe-back satin
- 18 x 22-inch piece lightweight sheer fusible interfacing (Perfect Fuse Sheer)
- 3 yards gold lamé piping, or 3 yards ⅛-inch-diameter cotton cable cord and 1 package gold lamé bias tape
- 4 (3-inch-long, excluding hanging loop) gold tassels or 2 skeins gold metallic embroidery floss
- ⅔ yard gold cord for hanging loops
- 8 x 9-inch piece template plastic
- Water-soluble marking pen
- Embroidery designs, approximately 3½ inches in length and width (OESD designs shown)
- Rayon embroidery thread in desired colors
- Bobbin thread for embroidery
- All-purpose thread to match fabric
- Liquid embroidery stabilizer (Perfect Sew)
- Polyester fiberfill
- Basic sewing tools and equipment

Cutting
- Enlarge the diamond shape on page 101 on template plastic and mark the center. Use a large needle to pierce the center to make a hole for centering purposes.
- From the satin, cut two 18 x 22-inch pieces. Use the template to cut four diamonds from one piece and set them aside for the ornament backs. Apply liquid stabilizer to the remaining 18 x 22-inch piece and allow to dry thoroughly. Press to remove any wrinkles.
- Apply the fusible interfacing to the wrong side of the stabilized rectangle.

Embroidery & Assembly

1. Use the water-soluble marker to draw around the template four times on the right side of the stabilized and interfaced satin. Mark the center point of each diamond, and then draw a centering axis on each one. Be sure to allow room for hooping (Figure 1).

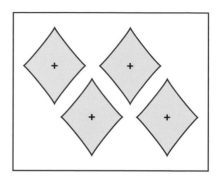

Figure 1
Draw around diagonal template on fabric right side.

Marta's Tassel Trick

Can't find tassels in the right size or color? Make your own using embroidery floss with Marta's quick and clever method. You will need one skein of gold metallic embroidery floss to make two 3-inch-long tassels. Refer to the photo.

1. Leave the paper wrap on the skein of floss.

2. Find the end and pull out 16 inches of floss; cut off and cut into two 8-inch pieces.

3. Thread an 8-inch length of floss through the loops at each end of the skein. Bring the ends together and tie an overhand knot 1 inch from the skein end. Trim the excess floss ½ inch from the knot.

4. Wrap excess floss from step 3 around looped end, ½ inch below end. Secure with fabric adhesive.

5. Cut through the center of the skein for two identical tassels.

2. Hoop the satin and embroider the desired designs. If desired, wash the completed embroideries to remove the stabilizer and press. However, it is not necessary to do this since the stabilizer adds desirable firmness to the completed ornaments.

3. Cut out each diamond shape around embroidery. If pieces have been washed, center the template over each embroidery and redraw outer edge; cut out.

4. If ready-made gold piping is not available, make piping by wrapping the gold lamé bias tape around the cotton cord and stitching close to the cord with a zipper foot (Figure 2).

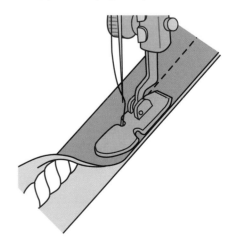

Figure 2
Make piping.

5. Pin piping to each embroidered diamond, beginning and ending at the upper point and clipping the piping seam allowance as needed at the points. Stitch close to cord.

6. Cut four 6-inch-long pieces of gold cord and knot the ends of each piece together with an overhand knot (Figure 3).

Figure 3
Make overhand knot at cord ends.

7. Position a loop at the upper point of each ornament front and stitch in place. Pin a tassel loop at the bottom point and stitch in place. To make your own tassels, see Marta's Tassel Trick on page 100.

8. With right sides facing, stitch each ornament front to a back; leave a 2½-inch-long opening on one side for turning. Stitch with the wrong side of the ornament front facing you so you can see the previous piping stitching. Stitch just inside the first stitching.

9. Turn the ornaments right side out and slipstitch the opening closed. ✦

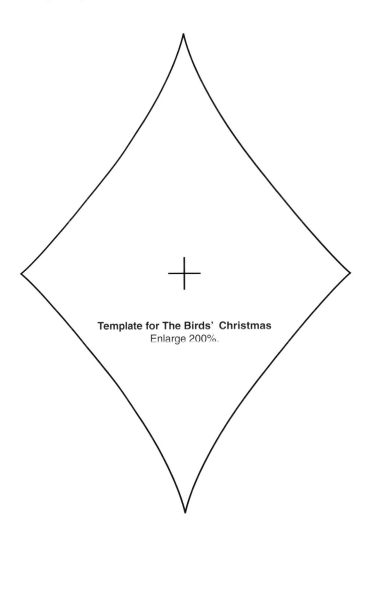

Template for The Birds' Christmas
Enlarge 200%.

Christmas Framed

Design by Carol Zentgraf

Frame a favorite embroidered motif (or a purchased or handmade Christmas appliqué, or a piece of Christmas needlework) in this layered wool felt pillow. Felt doesn't ravel, making it ideal for decorative cut edges to set off the center panel and the colored layers.

Finished Size
21 inches square including the flange beyond the 18-inch-square pillow form

Materials
- ⅔ yard each red, white and green wool felt (at least 54 inches wide
- 18-inch-square pillow form
- Embroidery designs: 5-inch-diameter wreath and 2-inch-diameter holly motif, or substitute similarly sized ready-made Christmas (or other holiday-themed) appliqués
- ⅝-inch-wide paper-backed fusible web strips
- Tear-away stabilizer
- All-purpose thread to match fabrics
- Rayon machine-embroidery thread and bobbin thread
- Air- or water-soluble marking pen
- Rotary cutter with decorative blade
- Rotary cutter, mat and ruler
- Press cloth
- Basic sewing tools and equipment

Cutting
Note: *Cut all squares using the rotary cutter with decorative blade.*

- From the red felt, cut one 15¼-inch square.
- From the white felt, cut one 16½-inch square.
- From the green felt, cut one 21-inch square for the pillow front and two 14 x 21-inch rectangles for the pillow back.
- From the tear-away stabilizer, cut five 8-inch squares.

Assembly
1. Use the marking pen to draw perpendicular lines at the center of the white felt square. Center

a piece of the tear-away stabilizer on the wrong side of the felt and place the felt and stabilizer in the embroidery-machine hoop. Embroider the chosen embroidery design and then carefully tear away the excess stabilizer on the back of the work after removing it from the hoop.

Note: If you are using a ready-made appliqué or piece of needlework in lieu of embroidering on the felt, use temporary spray adhesive to adhere it to the felt and then stitch in place by hand or machine using the appropriate technique for the appliqué.

2. To embroider the holly motifs on the red square, mark centering points for each corner as shown in Figure 1.

Figure 1
Mark 4½" from each corner
for holly embroidery placement.

3. Embroider each motif as described for embroidering on the white felt (or sew appliqués in place instead). Use the fabric marker to draw a 6-inch square on point in the center of the red felt square as shown in Figure 2. Use the rotary cutter with decorative blade to cut out the square.

Figure 2
Mark 6" square in red felt center. Cut out.

4. On the wrong side of the red felt square, position and apply fusible web strips along the center opening edges and at the outer edges (Figure 3).

Figure 3
Apply fusible web tape to wrong
side around opening and outer edges.

5. Remove the backing paper and center the red felt square on the white felt square, making certain the embroidery (or appliqué) is centered in the opening. Cover with a press cloth and fuse the edges in place following the manufacturer's directions. Topstitch close to the center and outer cut edges of the red square.

6. Apply fusible web to the wrong side of the white felt square close to the outer edges. Remove the paper backing, center the square on the green square. Fuse as you did for the first square.

7. For the back of the pillow cover, overlap the green felt rectangles to make a 20½-inch square (Figure 4). Baste the overlapping edges together.

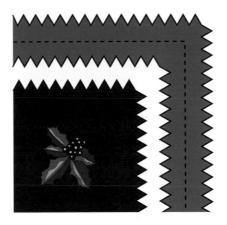

Figure 5
Stitch 1¼" from outer edges.

9. Insert the pillow form through the overlapping back edges. ✦

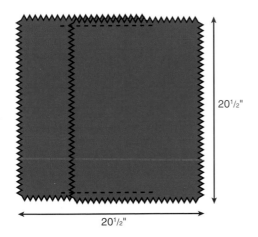

20½"

20½"

Figure 4
Overlap and baste layers together.

8. With wrong sides facing, sew the front and back covers together, stitching 1¼ inches from the outer edges (Figure 5). Remove the basting.

Snowmen on Ice

Design by Judith Sandstrom

Frosty men with jaunty plaid scarves "skate" on thin ice in this wintry little lap quilt. If desired, add embroidered facial features and a jaunty black top hat to one or more snowmen.

Finished Size

54½ x 69½ inches

Materials

- 44/45-inch-wide cotton quilting fabric
  - ¼ yard each 4 different blue prints
  - ⅜ yard each 2 additional blue prints
  - 1¾ yards white tone-on-tone print for snowmen appliqués
  - 1 yard red/green even plaid
  - ½ yard blue print for binding
  - 3½ yards backing fabric
- 58 x 73-inch piece thin cotton batting
- Paper-backed fusible web
- Template plastic or white paper
- Tear-away stabilizer
- All-purpose sewing thread in dark green and white
- Rotary cutter, mat and ruler
- ¼-inch presser foot
- Optional: quilting thread and needles for hand quilting
- Basic sewing tools and equipment

Cutting

- Launder and iron all fabrics before cutting.
- From each of the blue prints, cut one 6½ x 44-inch strip. From each strip, cut four 6½ x 9½-inch rectangles for a total of 24 blue rectangles.
- From any remaining blue fabric, cut two 6½-inch squares and two 3½ x 6½-inch rectangles.
- From the white tone-on-tone print, cut (14) 3½ x 44-inch strips and set nine strips aside. From the remaining five strips, cut a total of (27) 3½ x 6½-inch rectangles.
- From the plaid, cut seven 3½ x 44-inch strips for the borders and one 3 x 24-inch strip for Scarf A.
- Trace the scarf A template on page 110 onto template plastic or white paper and cut out. Fold the 3 x 24-inch plaid strip in half lengthwise with right sides facing and pin. Position the template for Scarf A at the fold and trace around it seven times (Figure 1 on page 108). Attach the ¼-inch presser foot and stitch ¼ inch from all but the upper edge of each Scarf A. Cut out along the traced lines. Turn right side out and press.

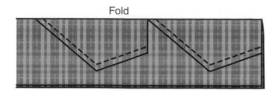

Figure 1
Trace 7 Scarf A on folded plaid strip.
Stitch ¼" from lines and cut out.

Figure 2
Center snowman on block. Add scarf pieces and fuse.

• Trace seven of the Scarf B template on page 110 onto the paper side of the fusible web. Leave ½ inch of space between the shapes. Apply the fusible web with tracings to the wrong side of the plaid and cut out along the traced lines.

• Using the template on page 110, trace seven of the snowman shape onto the paper side of fusible web with at least ½ inch between the shapes. Cut the snowmen in one large section from the fusible web; apply the section to the wrong side of the white tone-on-tone print. Cut out each snowman along the traced lines.

• From the binding fabric, cut seven 2 x 44-inch strips.

• Cut the backing fabric into two equal lengths and sew the two pieces together. Press the seam allowance to one side and set the back aside.

Quilt Top Assembly

Note: *Use ¼-inch-wide seam allowances.*

1. From the two darkest blue fabrics from which you cut rectangles, choose seven 6½ x 9½-inch rectangles. These will be the background pieces for the snowmen.

2. Remove the paper backing from each snowman and each plaid Scarf B piece. Center each snowman on a blue rectangle. Position Scarf B at the neck and tuck the raw edge of Scarf A ⅛ inch under the Scarf B section with the bottom point toward the bottom of the snowman. Fuse in place following the manufacturer's directions (Figure 2).

3. Cut seven pieces of tear-away stabilizer slightly larger than the snowman motif. Place one piece under each rectangle behind the snowman and pin in place.

4. Thread the machine with white thread and adjust for a medium-width zigzag stitch. Stitch each snowman to its background block. Pull the threads to the back of the blue rectangle; knot securely and trim ends.

5. Using the dark green thread, stitch around each Scarf B; pull thread to the back of the rectangle, knot and trim. Carefully remove the stabilizer behind the appliqué.

6. Refer to Figure 3 for steps 6–10. Arrange the snowman blocks with the remaining blue rectangles and squares and the 3½ x 6½-inch white rectangles to form five vertical rows. Sew the pieces together in each row and press all seams toward the blue fabric.

7. Cut each of three 3¼ x 44-inch white strips into two equal lengths (six half-strips). Stitch each half-strip to one of the remaining white strips for a total of six long sashing strips.

8. Trim each sashing strip to 63½ inches long. Arrange the strips in alternating fashion with the snowman strips and sew together. Press the seams toward the snowman strips.

9. Stitch four of the plaid border strips together in pairs to make two long strips, taking care to match the plaid. Press the seam in one direction in each strip. Trim each strip to 63½ inches and sew to opposite long sides of the quilt top. Press the seams toward the borders.

10. Cut one of the remaining plaid strips in half and then sew each half-strip to a remaining plaid border strip. Trim each strip to 54½ inches; sew a strip to the top and bottom edge of the quilt. Press the seams toward the borders as shown by the arrows (Figure 3).

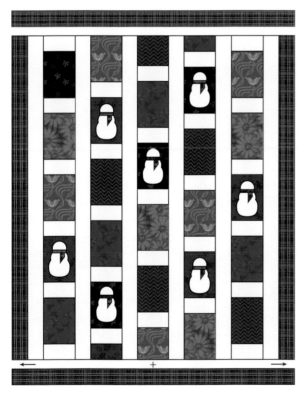

Figure 3
Add side borders and then
top and bottom borders.

Quilt Finishing

1. Place the backing facedown on a large flat surface and center the batting on top. Arrange the completed quilt top, faceup, on top of the batting; hand- or pin-baste the layers together.

2. Hand- or machine-quilt as desired. The quilt shown was hand-quilted ¼ inch from the seam line on each blue rectangle and square.

Note: *If desired, you can simply stitch in the ditch of all vertical and horizontal seam lines to "set" the quilt and then stitch around the snowmen.*

3. Trim the excess batting and backing even with the quilt top edge and remove all basting.

4. Using bias seams as shown in Figure 4, sew the binding strips together to make one long strip. Cut one end on the bias and then turn under and press ¼ inch. Fold the strip in half with wrong sides facing and press.

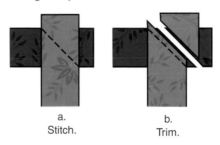

a.
Stitch.

b.
Trim.

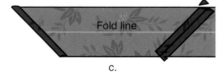

c.
Press. Trim seam allowance "ears."

d.
Fold and press.
Figure 4
Join binding strips and press.

5. Beginning somewhere below the center on one long edge of the quilt and using a ¼-inch-wide seam allowance, sew the binding to the quilt. Begin stitching 2 inches from the turned end, and when you reach the beginning point, trim the excess binding, leaving enough to tuck into the open end of the binding. Complete the stitching.

Note: Miter the corners as you reach them.

6. Turn the binding to the wrong side of the quilt around the seam allowance and slipstitch in place along the stitching line, mitering the corners as you reach them. ✦

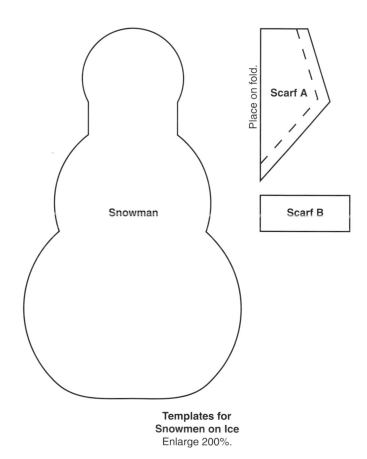

Snowman

Place on fold.

Scarf A

Scarf B

Templates for Snowmen on Ice
Enlarge 200%.

Set the Holiday Table

Dressing your table for the holidays can be just as much fun as choosing your own holiday attire. Look ahead for ways to decorate your holiday table: An easy-to-sew reversible runner, a set of fun place mats with coordinating napkins, or stocking-shaped silverware holders that can double as gifts are just a few of the projects to stitch for your table.

Holiday Reverses

Design by Stephanie Corina Goddard

Create a festive table runner with a split personality. Redecorating the table for the next holiday is as simple as flipping this reversible patchwork runner fashioned from fabrics in colors for two seasons.

Finished Size

16½ x 80 inches with a 24-inch-wide center star panel

Materials

- 44/45-inch-wide cotton fabric:
    - ⅜ yard red for Christmas star
    - ⅜ yard silver for New Year's star
    - ¾ yard gold for star background (appears on both sides)
    - ¼ yard each 5 Christmas prints to coordinate with red star color and gold background
    - ¼ yard each 5 different silver and gold winter prints to coordinate with silver star color and gold background
    - ⅜ yard gold print for binding (appears on both sides)
- 1½ yards 45-inch-wide needle-punched craft fleece
- Pattern tracing paper or cloth
- Fabric marking pencil
- Rotary cutter, mat and ruler
- Basic sewing tools and equipment

Cutting

- To prepare a pattern for the gold setting triangles, fold a 4½ x 16½-inch rectangle of pattern tracing paper or cloth in half crosswise and place a ruler as shown in Figure 1. Cut.

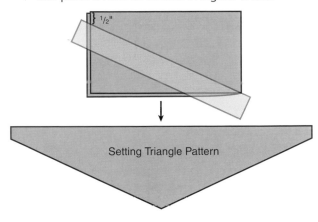

Figure 1
Position ruler on folded paper rectangle.

- From the red and from the silver fabrics for the stars, cut one 8½-inch square and four 4⅞-inch squares of each color.
- From the gold background fabric, cut eight 4½-inch squares and eight 4⅞-inch squares. Use the pattern to cut four setting triangles.

• From each of the 10 prints, cut two 7 x 16½-inch rectangles.
• From the binding fabric, cut five 2½-inch-wide strips.
• From the craft fleece, cut two 16½ x 32½-inch rectangles; set the remaining fleece aside. Using the setting-triangle pattern piece as your guide, trim one end of each rectangle to a point.

Assembly

Note: *Use ¼-inch-wide seam allowances unless otherwise directed.*

1. Place each 4⅞-inch star square face down on the right side of a 4⅞-inch gold background square. Draw a diagonal line on the gold square from upper left to lower right, and then stitch ¼ inch from the line on each side. Cut on the diagonal line (Figure 2).

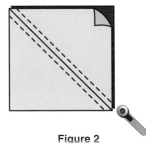

Figure 2
Draw a diagonal line on the gold square in each pair. Stitch ¼" from the line; cut apart.

2. Gently press each square open, pressing the seam toward the red or silver fabric in each resulting triangle pair (Figure 3). You should have eight half-square triangles of each color combination.

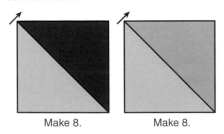

Make 8.   Make 8.

Figure 3
Press seams toward red and silver triangles.

3. Referring to Figure 4, arrange the pieces for each star into rows. Sew the pieces together in rows and press the seams in the direction of the arrows. Sew the rows together to complete the block and press the seams toward the large center square.

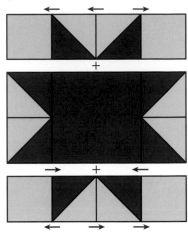

Figure 4
Block Assembly

4. Add a setting triangle to opposite sides of each square and press the seam toward the triangle (Figure 5).

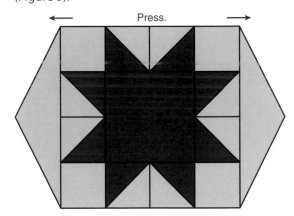

Figure 5
Add setting triangles to each star block.

5. From the remaining fleece, cut a piece an inch or so larger all around than the star with triangles. Place one of the patchwork pieces face up on top and smooth into place, taking care to keep the block square. Pin-baste the layers together and

then machine-baste a scant ¼ inch from the raw edges of the block. Trim the fleece even with the block raw edges.

6. Pin the remaining patchwork piece to the opposite side with all raw edges matching.

7. From each set of colors, choose a 7 x 16½-inch rectangle and sandwich one straight edge of the star unit between them. Stitch through all layers (Figure 6).

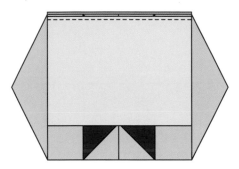

Figure 6
Sandwich 1 straight edge of patchwork
between 2 rectangles. Stitch.

8. Adjust the sewing machine for a wide zigzag stitch. Butt the short end of one 16½ x 32-inch fleece rectangle to the seam edge and zigzag the layers together (Figure 7).

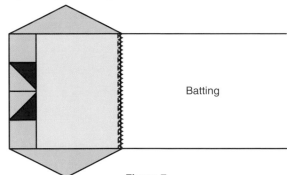

Batting

Figure 7
Butt 16½" x 32" fleece rectangle
to pieced unit. Zigzag over edges.

9. Beginning on either side, flip the panel into finished position, smooth it over the fleece and pin. Turn the work over. Flip, smooth and pin the second panel in place through all layers, and then

remove the pins from the first side you pinned. Make sure that all raw edges are even with batting edges. Working from the pinned side, machine-baste through all layers a scant ¼ inch from the long raw edge of the fabric rectangle (Figure 8).

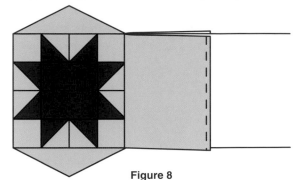

Figure 8
Flip front and back rectangles into place.
Machine-baste a scant ¼" from raw edges.

10. Choose the next rectangle for each side of the runner. Beginning on one side, pin the appropriate fabric panel to the runner with long raw edges aligned. Flip the panel and add the other rectangle to the opposite side, pinning through all layers. Stitch ¼ inch from the fabric raw edges and make sure that both fabric layers have been caught in the stitching.

11. Flip the panels into position. Pin, baste and then add the next panel in the sequence. Continue until the fleece rectangle is covered with fabric. After adding the fifth rectangle, flip only one of the two just added into position on the fleece and pin in place. Turn over to expose the fleece and trim the fabric even with the shaped end of the fleece (Figure 9).

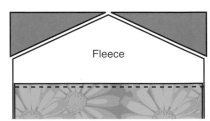

Fleece

Figure 9
Trim one rectangle even with
shaped end of fleece panel.

12. Flip the remaining fabric into place, pin in place over the pointed end and trim in the same manner. Machine-baste a scant ¼ inch from the fabric raw edges through all layers (Figure 10).

Figure 10
Trim remaining rectangle
even with fleece shaped end.

13. Repeat steps 8–12 to zigzag the remaining piece of batting to the opposite end of the patchwork and cover it with fabrics. Take care to use the same fabrics in the same positions on both sides of the runner when completing the second half.

Finishing

1. Use bias seams to join the 2½-inch-wide binding strips to make one long strip. Press the seams open and cut one end at a 45-degree angle. Turn under and press ¼ inch. Fold the strip in half lengthwise with wrong sides facing and raw edges aligned; press.

2. Beginning with the turned end at least an inch or more below the inward corner of the patchwork as shown in Figure 11, pin and stitch the binding to the runner. Begin stitching at least 1 inch from the open, turned end of the binding strip.

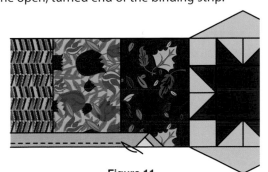

Figure 11
Pin and stitch binding to runner edges;
miter corners when you reach them.

Note: *When you reach the inward corners, stretch the binding taut for ¾ inch around the corner so that it will lie flat when turned.*

3. Miter the points when you reach them (Figure 12).

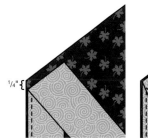

Figure 12
Miter each outside point by pinning to within ¼" of the corner. Fold the binding back on itself ¼"; then continue pinning. Stitch.

4. When you reach the beginning of the binding, trim the excess, leaving enough to tuck into the folded end. Complete the stitching.

5. Wrap the binding over the seam allowance to the other side of the runner and hand-sew in place, mitering the corners as you reach them. Alternatively, pin the binding in place and stitch in the ditch from the first side to catch the underlayer in the stitching. ✦

Plan It Two Ways

Plan two colorways that reflect your family's interests, but remember that the same binding appears on both sides. For mix-and-match options, consider two different holidays such as Thanksgiving, Christmas, Hanukkah, Kwanzaa or New Year's. Or, select two themes from the vast range of colors and print styles that all say "Christmas." Choose traditional reds and greens, Victorian colors, fashion colors, sophisticated prints or juvenile motifs. Make a set of napkins from the prints from each side. Cut 18-inch squares and finish the outer edges on the serger with a rolled edge in a matching or contrasting color.

Crazy for Christmas

Designs by Janis Bullis

Tuck flatware into crazy-patch stockings that can double as ornaments, and then set the table with colorful matching place mats and napkins. It all adds up to a brightly hued holiday setting for sharing the fun and frivolity of the season.

Finished Sizes

Place Mat: 12 x 18 inches
Stocking: 5 x 10 inches
Napkin: 16 inches square

Materials for One Three-Piece Place Setting

- 44/45-inch-wide washable linen or linen/cotton-blend fabric:
    - ⅝ yard gold
    - ½ yard each red and green
    - ¼ yard each royal blue and purple
- ¼ yard each 5 different narrow decorative ribbons
- All-purpose thread to match fabrics and ribbons
- 3 yards filler cord for matching piping or 3 yards purchased piping in a color that matches or coordinates with the fabric color(s)
- Pattern tracing cloth
- 14 x 20-inch rectangle lightweight quilt batting
- ⅜ yard red cotton for stocking lining
- ¼ yard ⅝-inch-wide red grosgrain ribbon for hanging loop
- Temporary spray adhesive
- Several small coordinating buttons and/or other embellishments
- Zipper foot
- Point presser
- Basic sewing tools and equipment

Cutting

- Enlarge patterns for stocking, place mat center and place mat frame as directed on page 123. Use the patterns to cut the required pieces as directed.
- From the red linen, cut one stocking back and one place mat border. Cut one 13 x 19-inch rectangle for the place mat back. Set the remaining fabric aside for the patchwork.
- From the gold linen, cut one 20-inch square for the napkin. Save the remainder for the patchwork.
- From the green fabric, cut four 1⅛ x 26-inch true-bias strips for the piping. Set the scraps aside for the patchwork.
- From the red cotton for the stocking lining, cut two stockings.

Crazy Patchwork Assembly

Note: Use ¼-inch-wide seams.

1. Begin by cutting each color fabric in roughly 4–6-inch shapes with odd angles (Figure 1).

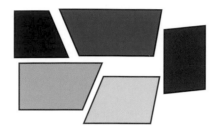

Figure 1
Cut assorted shapes from each of the five colors.

2. Combining colors at random and using ¼-inch-wide seam allowances, stitch pieces together in pairs. Press the seam allowance open in each pair. Stitch two pairs or single pieces together with seams perpendicular to each other (Figure 2).

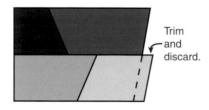

Figure 2
Sew pairs together to create center.

3. Mark and trim on the edge of the resulting piece at a new angle (Figure 3).

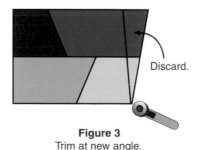

Figure 3
Trim at new angle.

4. Add a third pair (Figure 4). Continue to add fabric pieces working from the center out to create a 14 x 20-inch piece of patchwork for the place mat center and a 7 x 11-inch piece for the stocking. As the piece for the place mat center grows, you may need to join two pairs before adding them to the center. Anything goes with crazy piecing.

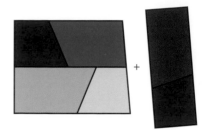

Figure 4
Add next pair; trim and discard excess.

5. Stitch decorative ribbons along some of the seam lines as desired to embellish the patchwork.

Place Mat Assembly

Note: Use ½-inch-wide seam allowances.

1. Staystitch the place mat border ⅜ inch from the inner raw edge. Fold the border in quarters to locate the centers and mark them with a ⅛-inch-long snip. Clip the inner rounded corners to the staystitching in ¼- or ½-inch increments (Figure 5).

Figure 5
Staystitch frame, mark centers and clip curves.

2. Fold the patchwork rectangle in half and then in half again and use the pattern for the place mat center to cut out the patchwork center. Before unfolding, make ⅛-inch-long snips to mark the centers.

3. With right sides facing and center snips matching all around, pin and stitch the frame to the patchwork center. Press the seam toward the frame. Topstitch close to the frame edge through all layers (Figure 6).

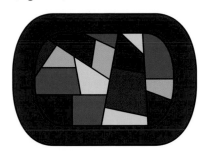

Figure 6
Press seam toward frame; topstitch.

4. Use the completed front as a pattern to trim the place mat back and batting rectangles to match. Apply a light coat of temporary spray adhesive to the wrong side of the place mat front and smooth in place on the batting. Machine-baste ¼ inch from the outer edge.

5. Sew the 1⅛ x 26-inch bias strips together with bias seams to make one long strip; press the seams open. Wrap the strip around the cable cord with wrong sides together and raw edges even. Attach the zipper foot and adjust it to the right of the needle. Stitch close to the cord to complete enough piping for the place mat and the stocking (Figure 7).

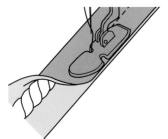

Figure 7
Stitch close to cord.

6. Thread the machine with a contrasting thread color in the bobbin and adjust the machine for a basting-length stitch. With raw edges even, pin and machine-baste the piping to the right side of

the place mat. To turn the curves, clip the piping seam allowance as needed. Leave a few inches of overlap where the piping ends meet. Make a neat join where the piping end meets the beginning as shown in Figure 8.

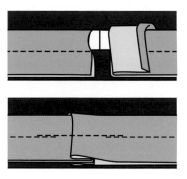

Figure 8
Join piping ends.

7. With right sides facing, pin the place mat back to the place mat front. With the back of the place mat front facing you, stitch just inside the basting stitching, leaving a 6-inch-long opening at one long edge for turning.

8. Turn the place mat right side out and turn in the opening edges. Slipstitch the edges together along the stitching line on the back of the mat. Press.

Stocking Assembly

1. Use the stocking pattern to cut one stocking from the patchwork. Apply piping to the outer edge as described for the place mat, beginning and ending at the upper edge.

2. With right sides facing, pin the stocking front to the stocking back. Stitch just inside the basting. Trim the seam allowance to ¼ inch and turn right side out.

3. With raw edges even, pin and machine-baste the remaining piping to the patchwork stocking upper edge. Join piping ends at the center back as described for the place mat and shown in Figure 8 above.

4. Fold the ribbon in half to make the hanging loop and baste in place at the upper edge on the stocking back, close to the back seam.

5. With right sides facing, pin and stitch the stocking lining pieces together. Leave a 4-inch-long opening in the back seam for turning (as shown in Figure 3 for Hanky-Panky Stockings on page 48). Trim the seam allowance to ¼ inch. Do not turn the lining right side out.

6. Tuck the stocking into the lining with right sides facing and upper raw edges aligned. Stitch just inside the basting around the upper edge. Turn the stocking right side out through the opening in the lining. Turn in and press the opening edges and topstitch the folded edges together. Tuck the completed lining inside the stocking.

Napkin With Mitered Hem
Note: *Follow the directions below to create a 16-inch-square napkin with 1-inch-wide double hems with mitered corners. If you prefer a 17-inch-square napkin, turn and press a double ½-inch-wide hem and topstitch. For an 18-inch-square napkin, finish the outer edges with a serged rolled edge.*

1. On one edge of the napkin square, turn under and press 1 inch. Turn under again and press to create a double hem. Repeat at the remaining three edges.

2. On one corner, open out the folds and refold on the diagonal with right sides together and cut edges aligned. Draw a 45-degree-angle stitching line as shown in Figure 9 and stitch from the diagonal fold to the hemline fold line. Back-tack at the beginning and end of the stitching. Trim the corner to within ¼ inch of the stitching. Press the seam open over a point presser. Repeat with the remaining corners.

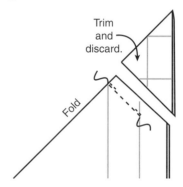

Figure 9
Fold on diagonal and stitch on
diagonal from fold to fold line.

3. Turn the corners to the inside following the original crease lines and press. Pin as needed. Stitch through all layers along the inner folded edges (Figure 10). ✦

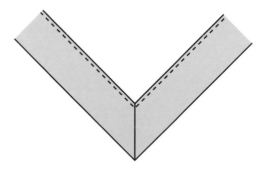

Figure 10
Turn double mitered hem to wrong side and stitch.

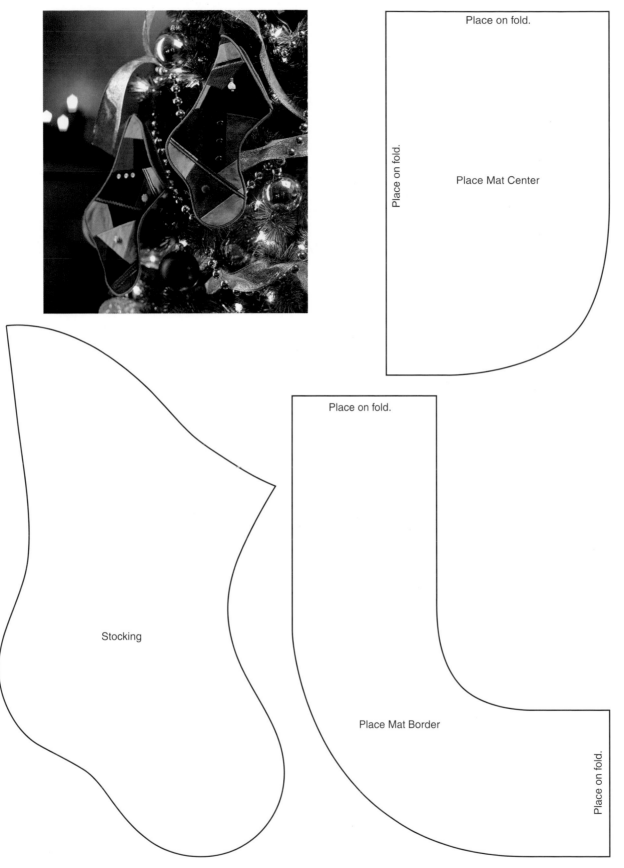

Place on fold.

Place on fold.

Place Mat Center

Place on fold.

Stocking

Place Mat Border

Place on fold.

Crazy for Christmas Patterns
Enlarge 200%.

Star Bright Place Setting

Designs by Janice Bullis

Fold and tuck a napkin inside the tree pocket on this clever place mat to create a star at the top and a ruffled tree skirt at the bottom. Star coasters add to this festive setting for casual holiday meals.

Finished Sizes
Place Mat: 12 x 18 inches
Coaster: 5 inches in diameter
Napkin: 16 inches square

Materials for One Place Setting
• 44/45-inch-wide tone-on-tone cotton prints:
    ½ yard red for place mat
    ⅝ yard gold for napkin and coaster
• 9 x 18-inch rectangle green tone-on-tone print for tree appliqué
• 14 x 26-inch rectangle lightweight cotton quilt batting
• 2 yards green extra-wide double-fold bias tape for binding
• ⅝ yard green maxi-piping for coaster
• 1 yard washable metallic trim
• All-purpose thread to match fabrics
• Template plastic

• Chalk marker
• Rotary cutter, mat and ruler
• Basic sewing tools and equipment

Cutting
• Wash and press all fabrics before proceeding to ensure washability.
• From red fabric, cut two 13 x 19-inch rectangles.
• Enlarge the tree templates A and B and the star template on page 129 as directed, and then trace them onto template plastic and cut out. Set aside tree template B for the appliqué placement later.
• Fold the green fabric in half with right sides facing and trace around tree template A. Cut out the double-layer tree.
• From gold fabric, cut one 20-inch napkin square. Trace and cut four stars.
• From batting, cut one 13 x 19-inch rectangle for the place mat; cut one star.

Place Mat & Coaster Assembly

1. Layer the place mat pieces with wrong sides facing and the batting rectangle in between. Use the chalk marker and rotary ruler to draw 30-degree-angle lines spaced 2 inches apart. Pin the layers together and then machine-stitch on the grid lines to quilt the layers together. Trim the quilted rectangle to 12 x 18 inches.

2. Using the edge of a bowl or plate, round off the corners of the place mat (Figure 1).

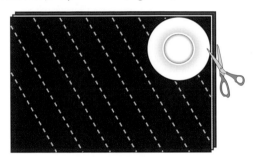

Figure 1
Draw quilting lines at a 30-degree
angle. Stitch. Round off corners.

3. With right sides facing, stitch the two trees together ¼ inch from the upper and lower edges only. Turn right side out and press (Figure 2).

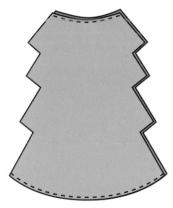

Figure 2
Stitch trees together at upper and lower edges only.

4. Position tree template B on the left side of the place mat and chalk-mark the outer edges. Position the fabric tree on the place mat with the long raw edges at the chalked lines; the tree will not lie flat on the mat to allow room for the folded napkin. Machine-baste ¼ inch from the raw edges. Cut the gold trim into 8-inch lengths and pin to the tree at the side edges, angling the trim across the tree. Pin in place and cut away any excess at each edge. Baste in place (Figure 3).

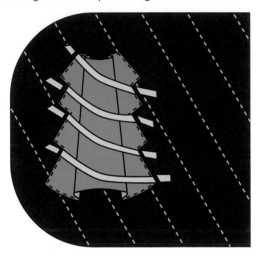

Figure 3
Machine baste tree and gold trim to place mat.

5. Satin-stitch over all raw edges of the tree (see Satin Stitching on page 127), catching the ends of the trim.

6. Bind the outer edge of the place mat with the ready-made bias tape. For a neat join, turn under the beginning end on the bias (Figure 4). When you reach the folded end, overlap and trim excess.

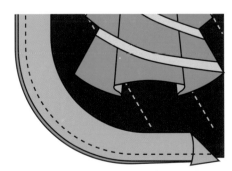

Figure 4
Open binding and turn end at an angle
at beginning of stitching for neat join.

7. On the wrong side of one star, draw a centerline from the point at the top to the bottom indent. With right sides facing, sew two stars together, stitching on the line and leaving the center 3 inches open. Backstitch at the points where the stitching stops and starts again (Figure 5).

Figure 5
Sew two stars together with 3" opening in center.

8. Open the stars to expose the opening in the center and press (Figure 6). Machine-baste ¼ inch from the raw edges.

Figure 6
Press star with wrong sides facing and slit in center.

9. With raw edges even and beginning near the center of a straight edge, pin and machine-baste piping to the right side of the star, making a neat join where the ends meet.

10. Layer the remaining stars wrong sides together with the batting star between them and machine-baste ¼ inch from the edges.

Satin Stitching

• Set your sewing machine for a medium to wide zigzag stitch with a very short length.
• Attach the zigzag, decorative or satin-stitch presser foot.
• Loosen the upper thread tension slightly or to the buttonhole setting indicator.
• Using small scraps of fabric, pin a fabric sample to a base-fabric sample to mimic the actual appliqué. Test your stitching on the sample before stitching the appliqué and adjust the stitches as needed. Guide the fabric to allow the right-hand swing of the needle to jump off the appliqué and the left-hand swing to penetrate the appliqué.
• Turn the assembly slowly and smoothly on curves to guide the appliqué edge so that it is always held at a 90-degree angle to the stitch width.
• For sharp angles, stop the machine with the needle penetrating the fabric, lift the presser foot and rotate the fabric sharply before lowering the foot and continuing to stitch.

11. Place the piped star face down on the layered stars and machine-stitch close to the cord in the piping, leaving a 2-inch-long opening in one straight section for turning (Figure 7). Turn right side out and press. Slipstitch the opening edge to the piping along the cord.

Figure 7
Machine-baste piped star to layered stars.

Napkin With Mitered Hem

Note: *Follow the directions at right to create a 16-inch-square napkin with 1-inch-wide double hems with mitered corners. If you prefer a 17-inch-square napkin, turn and press a double ½-inch-wide hem and topstitch. For an 18-inch-square napkin, finish the outer edges with a serged rolled edge.*

1. On one edge of the napkin square, turn under and press 1 inch. Turn under again and press to create a double hem. Repeat at the remaining three edges.

2. On one corner, open out the folds and refold on the diagonal with right sides together and cut edges aligned. Draw a 45-degree-angle stitching line as shown in Figure 8, and stitch from the diagonal fold to the hemline fold line. Back-tack at the beginning and end of the stitching. Trim the corner to within ¼ inch of the stitching. Press the seam open over a point presser. Repeat with the remaining corners.

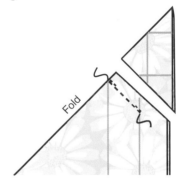

Figure 8
Stitch on line. Trim.

3. Turn the corners to the inside following the original crease lines and press. Pin as needed. Stitch through all layers along the inner folded edges (Figure 9).

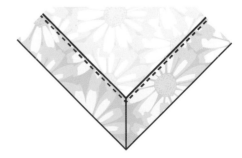

Figure 9
Turn hem to inside and edgestitch.

4. Accordion-fold the napkin and tuck under the tree. Fan out the upper and lower edges.
Note: *If desired, add small seasonal embellishments to the tree to resemble ornaments.* ✦

Star Coaster

Tree A

Tree B

Templates for Star Bright Tree
Enlarge 200%.

Pieced Elegance

Design by Carol Zentgraf

Dress your dining table for the holidays with this elegant pieced runner accented with decorative tassels. It's easy to make the runner longer or shorter to fit your table—simply add or omit one or more sections. Change fabrics and colors to suit your decorating theme for any special holiday during the year.

Finished Size
14 x 89 inches, excluding tassels

Materials
- 54-inch-wide home decor fabrics:
    - ¼ yard burgundy velvet (jacquard, embossed or printed)
    - ¼ yard gold velvet jacquard or tapestry
    - 1⅓ yards coordinating silk dupioni
- 2⅓ yards 1-inch-wide gold ribbon
- 1⅓ yards burgundy fringe with decorative header and beads
- ⅓ yard 6-inch-long bullion fringe for tassels
- 2 small wooden ornaments with flat base ¾–1 inch in diameter and a cord hanging loop
- Permanent fabric adhesive
- ¼-inch-wide fusible web tape for sheer fabrics
- Self-adhesive, double-sided basting tape
- Basic sewing tools and equipment

Cutting
- Cut one 8½ x 48-inch strip each from the burgundy velvet and gold fabric.
- From the silk dupioni, cut four 13 x 15-inch rectangles and two 15 x 46-inch rectangles.

Assembly
Note: *Use ½-inch-wide seam allowances.*

1. Sew the long edges of the burgundy velvet and gold fabrics together. Press the seam toward the darker of the two strips. Crosscut six 8-inch-wide segments from the strip unit (Figure 1 on page 132).

2. Sew two pieced segments together, alternating colors, as shown in Figure 2 on page 132. Repeat to make three pieced units. Press the seam allowances in one direction.

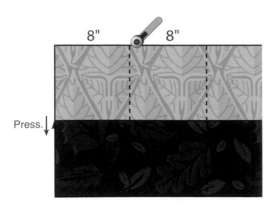

Figure 1
Crosscut 6 (8"-wide) segments from the strip unit.

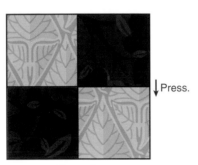

Figure 2
Make 3 pieced segments.

3. Following the manufacturer's directions, apply the fusible web tape to both long edges of the wrong side of the gold ribbon. Cut the ribbon into four equal lengths. Remove the paper backing from the tape and fuse the ribbon strips diagonally across two of the silk dupioni rectangles (Figure 3). Flip the pieces over and trim the excess ribbon even with the outer edges of the rectangle.

Figure 3
Fuse ribbons to each silk rectangle. Make 2.

4. Arrange the pieced units and ribbon panels in alternating fashion and sew together along the 15-inch edges. Press the seams toward the ribbon panels (Figure 4).

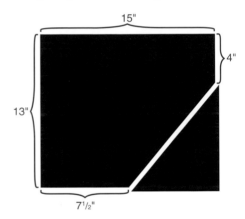

Figure 4
Sew pieces together. Press seams toward ribbon panels.

5. Referring to Figure 5, mark cutting lines on the remaining silk panels. Cut along the marked lines.

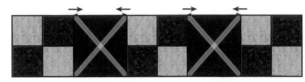

Figure 5
Draw cutting lines on remaining silk rectangles. Cut on lines.

6. Sew the end panels to the runner along the straight edges and press the seams open.

7. To make the runner back, sew the short ends of the 15 x 46-inch silk rectangles together, leaving 4 inches open in the center of the seam. Press the seam allowances to one side.

8. Apply self-adhesive, double-sided basting tape along the edges of the pieced runner on the right side. Center the runner on the runner back with right sides facing. Remove the basting tape backing paper a short section at a time, and adhere the runner top to the back making sure the layers remain smooth.

9. With the pieced runner facing you, draw stitching lines ½ inch from the raw edges at each pointed end. Stitch the layers together ½ inch from the long raw edges of the runner top and along the marked stitching lines at the point (Figure 6).

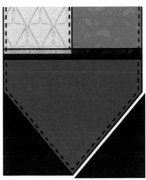

Figure 6
Stitch pieced runner to back
panel. Trim ends even with runner.

10. Trim the back even with the pieced panel edges at the pointed ends. Turn the runner right side out through the opening in the center seam. Press all edges, and then slipstitch the opening edges together.

11. Cut two 17-inch lengths of the beaded fringe. Center and glue the fringe to the end seams of the runner, wrapping the trim ends to the back.

12. Make and attach a decorative tassel to each pointed end of the runner as directed in Tassel Time at right. ✦

Tassel Time

1. From the bullion and the burgundy beaded fringe, cut a 6-inch length for each tassel.

2. Apply glue to the bullion fringe header and roll up tightly.

3. Wrap and glue the beaded fringe around the header of the bullion fringe.

4. Glue the ornament to the top of the rolled fringe and allow to dry thoroughly.

5. Cut the top of the ornament hanging loop. Thread a needle with one end of the hanging loop and stitch through the runner point from front to back. Repeat with the other end of the hanging loop, stitching ¼ inch from the first loop. Knot the loop ends together several times on the back of the runner and apply glue to the knot to secure.

Oh, Tannenbaum!

Designs by Karen Dillon

Search your stash for just the right fabric scraps and trims for these pretty Christmas trees. Make several to group on the mantel or to use for table centerpieces. *Beautifully Beribboned* is a great way to use up scraps from your stash. For a more formal approach, embellish a velvet tree by covering with beads and silk flowers to create *Christmas Glamour*.

Finished Size
Christmas Glamour: 12 inches tall, excluding base and tree topper
Beautifully Beribboned: 12 inches tall, excluding base and tree topper

Materials for Basic Tree & Cover
• ⅜ yard 44/45-inch-wide fabric of choice (burgundy velvet or green cotton)
• Pattern tracing cloth or paper (with 1-square-to-the-inch grid)
• All-purpose thread to match fabric
• 12-inch-tall plastic foam tree form
• Point presser or seam roll
• Staple gun or permanent fabric adhesive
• 4-inch-diameter cardboard circle
• Basic sewing tools and equipment

Tree Cover Cutting & Assembly
1. Enlarge the pattern (Figure 1) on gridded pattern tracing cloth or paper and cut out.

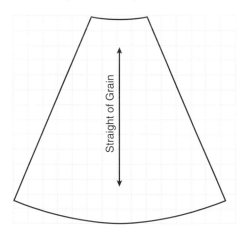

Figure 1
Tree Cover Pattern
1 square = 1"

2. Use the pattern to cut one tree cover from the desired fabric.

3. Fold the cover in half with right sides facing and stitch ⅜ inch from the long raw edges (Figure 2). Press the seam open over a point presser or seam roll.

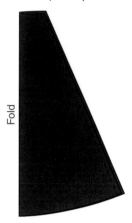

Fold

Figure 2
Fold tree cover in half and
stitch ³/₈" from long edges.

4. Turn the cover right side out and hand-baste close to the upper raw edge; leave the needle and thread attached. Repeat 1 inch from the lower edge. Slip the cover over the tree form. It should be a snug fit. Draw up the stitches at the top to fit, and stitch in place several times for a neat closure. You will cover the raw edges with the tree topper. Draw up the stitches around the bottom for a snug fit and tie off securely. Optional: Staple in place close to the raw edges or use fabric adhesive for added security.

5. Using the cardboard circle as a pattern, draw a circle on the wrong side of the remaining fabric, adding ½ inch beyond the cardboard edge. Cut out.

6. Apply fabric adhesive around the outer edge of the cardboard and wrap the excess fabric over the edge and smooth into the adhesive. Allow to dry. Use fabric adhesive to glue the completed base to the bottom of the tree with the cardboard against the plastic foam. Allow to dry.

7. Embellish the tree as desired (see below for the two versions shown).

Christmas Glamour

Materials
• Embellishments
    1 stem silk hydrangea (with at least
      18 blossoms)
    ⅛ yard green organza
    4 x 20-inch-wide strip paper-backed
      fusible web
    1 yard iridescent pearl chain
    Clear beaded floral stem
    Green beaded floral stem
    20 seed beads
    20 sequins
• 2 small dishes for beads and sequins
• 1-inch-long sequin pins
• 4-inch-long hat pin
• Assorted beads in various sizes for tree topper
• Pliers
• Optional: Gold metal candle stand for tree base

Assembly
1. Pour the beads into a dish; repeat with sequins.

2. Cut two 4 x 20-inch pieces of organza and fuse together with the lightweight fusible web following the manufacturer's directions. Cut 6–8 leaves from the double-layer organza using the leaf template on page 138.

3. Remove 18 blossoms from the hydrangea stem. Use pliers to remove the center of each flower.

4. Load a sequin pin with a seed bead, followed by a sequin. Insert the beaded pin through the hole in a flower. Repeat with all remaining flowers.

5. Position three beaded blossoms with a leaf toward the top of the tree and push the pins into the form. Add the remaining blossoms in

groups of three, rearranging as needed to create a pleasing design.

6. Drape the pearl chain around the tree and pin in place with sequin pins. Fill in the design with bead clusters, using pins to secure them.

7. Arrange assorted beads on the hat pin for the tree topper and stick into the top of the tree.

8. Optional: Set the completed tree on the candle stand base.

Beautifully Beribboned

Materials
- ½ yard each ¼–½-inch-wide ribbons; choose assorted colors and styles
- ⅜-inch-diameter sequins in assorted colors, 1 for each bow
- Seed beads
- 1-inch-long sequin pins
- Gold Christmas ball removed from a Christmas floral pick
- Pipe cleaner and glue for insert in tree topper
- Optional: Gold metal candle stand for tree base

Assembly
1. Cut a total of 130 (6-inch-long) pieces of ribbon; trim ribbon ends on the bias.

2. Tie a single knot in the center of each ribbon.

3. Insert a sequin pin through a seed bead and then a sequin and then into the center of a bow.

4. Pin the bows into the covered tree, arranging in the desired manner. Trim ribbon ends as needed, especially on ribbons at the tree top, to keep things in proportion.

5. Insert the wire on the Christmas ball into the tree top. If it has no wire, glue a pipe cleaner inside.

6. Optional: Set the completed tree on the candle stand base. ✦

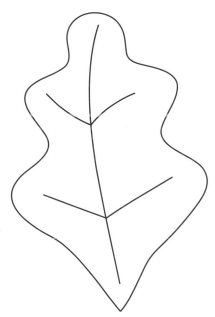

Template for Oh, Tannenbaum!
Actual Size

Dress for the Season

Dress up for the holidays with styles that range from casual to sophisticated. Wrap your shoulders in a ruffled shawl and carry a matching evening bag. Turn sweatshirts into fun jackets. Or, sew an eye-catching wool jacket embellished with fabric strips in Christmas colors.

Winter in Bloom

Design by Pat Nelson

Winter flowers cut from a seasonal cotton print bloom on the surface of this simple vest. Add glittery texture to all raw edges with free-motion stitching using metallic thread. The sewing is easy, and the results will garner rave reviews every time you wear your one-of-a-kind vest for holiday events.

Finished Size
Your size

Materials
- Vest pattern of your choice
- Pattern tracing paper or cloth to trace the pattern pieces
- Solid or tone-on-tone print cotton for upper vest (see Determine Yardage on page 142)
- Coordinating cotton check or stripe for lower vest (see Determine Yardage on page 142)
- ½ yard cotton check or stripe for binding
- Print for lining in yardage given on pattern, plus ½ yard for appliqués
- Lightweight cotton woven or weft-insertion fusible interfacing (enough to accommodate the vest fronts and back)
- 1 yard paper-backed fusible web
- All-purpose thread to match fabrics
- Gold metallic thread
- Size 60/2 bobbin-weight thread (white or a color similar to your fabrics)
- Size 90/14 metallic needle
- Darning foot, ¼-inch foot and zigzag foot
- Basic sewing tools and equipment

Cutting
- Wash the fabrics to preshrink; press to remove wrinkles.
- Preshrink the interfacing following the manufacturer's directions.
- Using the original vest pattern pieces, cut the vest fronts and back from the print lining and from the interfacing. Set the remaining print lining fabric aside for the appliqués.
- Using the tracing-paper patterns, cut the upper fronts and upper back from the solid or tone-on-tone print fabric.
- Cut the lower fronts and lower back from the checked or stripe fabric.

• From the binding fabric, cut enough 1¾-inch-wide bias strips to make one long piece of binding for the outer edges of the vest—approximately 5¼ yards.

Assembly

1. Place the front and back interfacing pieces on the ironing board, fusible resin side up. Place the

Determine Yardage

1. Refer to the illustration for the following steps. To make the upper and lower pattern pieces, trace two fronts and a complete back onto the pattern tracing paper or cloth and cut out along the stitching lines around all edges—unless the pattern you are using is designed for bound edges to begin with. Mark the center-front line on both front pieces.

2. Draw a gently curving line from side to side on the back tracing paper and label the pieces.

3. Overlap the two fronts on the center front line, pin in place, and draw a gently curving line from side to side, beginning and ending at the same places in the side seams as the back pattern piece. Label the pieces as shown.

4. Cut the patterns apart on the drawn lines and use the pieces to determine the required yardage for each of the two fabrics for the vest.

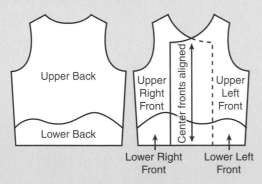

Pattern Preparation

upper and lower vest front and back pieces wrong side down on the interfacing pieces. Butt the upper and lower pieces together and fuse them to the interfacing following the manufacturer's directions (Figure 1).

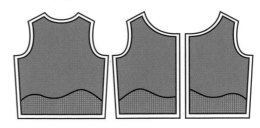

Figure 1
Position pieces on fusible
side of interfacing and fuse.

2. Insert the metallic needle in your sewing machine and thread the needle with the metallic thread. Fill a bobbin with the bobbin-weight thread. Attach the zigzag presser foot. Set up the machine for a normal straight stitch.

3. Fuse a scrap of fabric to a scrap of interfacing and do several rows of stitching to determine the desired stitch length and to ensure that the tension is properly adjusted for the threads. Adjust as needed so that no bobbin thread is pulled to the surface of the work.

4. Stitch meandering lines on the upper section of each vest piece (Figure 2).

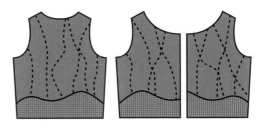

Figure 2
Stitch meandering lines on each piece.

5. Following the manufacturer's directions, apply fusible web to the wrong side of the print fabric set aside for the appliqués. Cut motifs from the fabric and arrange on the vest fronts and back as desired (Figure 3). Fuse in place.

Note: You can cut a single motif or several motifs and group them, overlapping pieces as desired to create your own unique appliqués as shown on the upper left shoulder.

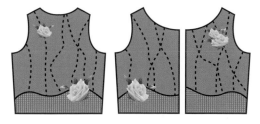

Figure 3
Position appliqués and fuse in place.

6. Adjust the machine for free-motion stitching by attaching the darning foot and dropping the feed dogs. Use metallic thread in the needle and bobbin thread in the bobbin. Using an irregular, side-to-side motion, move the vest under the needle as you stitch with a straight stitch over all raw edges (Figure 4). Begin by stitching over the raw edges at the curved lines where the upper and lower vest sections meet. Then cover the raw edges of the appliqués.

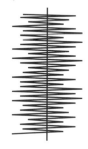

Figure 4
Use irregular free-motion zigzagging to cover raw edges.

7. Press the finished pieces; sew the lining pieces together at the shoulders and side seams and the vest pieces together in the same fashion. Press all seams open.

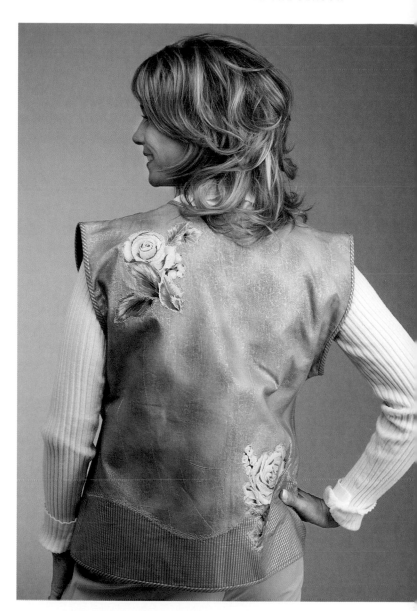

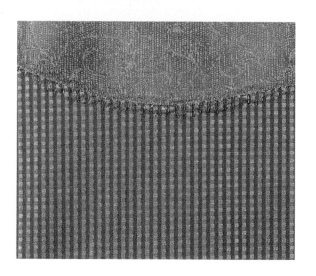

8. With wrong sides facing, pin the vest to the lining at all raw edges. Make sure the layers are flat and wrinkle-free. If the raw edges won't match perfectly without creating buckling in the layers, don't force them.

9. Sew the bias binding strips together with bias seams and press the seams open. Use to bind all raw edges of the vest, stitching ⅜ inch from the raw edges and wrapping the binding over the raw edges to the inside. Miter corners as you reach them and make a neat join where the binding ends meet at center back and around the armholes.

10. Sew buttons and buttonholes or snap fasteners as desired or directed in the pattern you have chosen. ✦

Tree-Time Top

Design by Karen Dillon

Easy appliqués and Christmas buttons turn a simple top into a favorite to wear for Christmas shopping, holiday luncheons with friends or cozy nights by the fire while you wrap gifts for those on your gift-giving list.

Finished Size
Your size

Materials
- Pattern for loose-fitting knit pullover top with set-in sleeves and jewel neckline
- Red knit in yardage specified on pattern
- 6 x 9-inch piece green tone-on-tone print for tree appliqué
- Scraps green solid or tone-on-tone print for the holly leaves
- 5 x 10-inch piece lightweight woven or weft-insertion fusible interfacing
- 12-inch-square piece lightweight paper-backed fusible web
- Pattern tracing paper or cloth
- Pencil
- 1 package wide, double-fold green bias tape for neckline
- 12-inch-long pieces 3 different narrow flexible braid trims (red, white and green) for tree garlands
- ¾ yard ½-inch-wide flexible-braid trim for neckline
- All-purpose sewing thread to match fabrics
- Green and gold topstitching thread
- Topstitching needle
- Tissue paper
- Assorted Christmas buttons
- 1 small star button for tree topper
- 12 (³⁄₁₆-inch) jingle bells
- 15 red ¼-inch buttons for holly berries
- 18–20 multicolor sequins and a matching-color bead for each one
- Liquid seam sealant
- Permanent fabric adhesive
- Open-toe presser foot
- Blind-hem presser foot
- Size 16 topstitching or jeans needle
- Size 16 twin needle
- Basic sewing tools and equipment

Cutting
- Trim away the neckline seam allowance on the shirt front and back pattern pieces (or clip the curves and turn under the seam allowances along the stitching lines to preserve the pattern for another use). Check the hem allowances. If they are not 1¼ inches wide on the sleeve and

shirt front and back pattern pieces, adjust the pattern so they are.

- Cut the shirt front, back and sleeves from the knit following the pattern guidesheet.
- Trace the neckline template on page 151 onto pattern tracing paper or cloth and cut out. Remove the tissue paper pattern piece from the

shirt front and pin the neckline template in place with the center front line at the fold and the shoulder line at the cut edge (Figure 1). Use the template as a guide to cut the shaped neckline. You may need to adjust it somewhat for the slope of the shoulder and the pattern size.

Figure 1
Re-shape front neckline.

- Use the front neckline template to cut a 1-inch-wide front neckline stabilizer from the lightweight woven or weft-insertion fusible interfacing. Use the back pattern piece as a guide to cut a 3-inch-wide stabilizer for the back neckline. Cut two 1-inch-wide strips of fusible interfacing along the length (the direction with little or no stretch), making them each the length of the shoulder seam.
- Cut a 6 x 9-inch piece of fusible web and trace the tree template on page 151 onto the paper side.
- Apply the fusible web to the green print following the manufacturer's directions. Cut out the tree and set aside.
- Using the template on page 151, trace 10 holly leaves onto the paper side of the remaining fusible web. Cut out each one with at least ⅛ inch excess beyond the line. Apply the pieces to the wrong side of the green scraps and cut out.

Assembly

1. Following the manufacturer's directions, apply the interfacing to the wrong side of the front and back necklines and to each front shoulder edge (Figure 2).

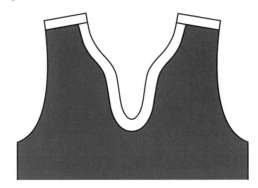

Figure 2
Apply fusible interfacing to front and back necklines and to front shoulders.

2. Stitch or serge both shoulder seams. Press open or toward the back.

3. To shape the bias to the neckline edge before sewing, position the folded edge of the bias tape along the cut neckline edge. Begin and end the tape somewhere close to one shoulder on the back of the shirt allowing for a turn-under and overlap. Steam-press the bias to shape it and shrink out as much fullness as possible in the upper edge at the center front curve. Allow the bias to dry thoroughly before applying it to the neckline.

Note: *The folded bias tape has one half that is slightly wider than the other. When shaping the tape and slipping it over the raw edge of the neckline for stitching, make sure that the narrower of the two halves is on the top.*

4. Slip the binding over the raw edge of the neckline and pin in place. Stitch along the inner folded edge, catching the underlayer in the stitching on the inside of the shirt (Figure 3). If you prefer, you can open the bias tape and stitch in the fold to attach it to the neckline; then wrap it to the inside and pin it in place before stitching in the ditch or along the bias edge from the right side, catching the inner layers in the stitching.

Figure 3
Slip shaped bias tape over neckline raw edge. Stitch.

5. Attach the twin needle and thread with the gold topstitching thread in the right needle and the green in the left needle. Adjust the machine for a zigzag stitch that is 2mm wide and 4mm long. Beginning at one shoulder seam, stitch around the neckline with the edge of the presser foot along the inner edge of the bias tape. Pull the thread tails through to the inside and tie off securely. Center the ½-inch-wide flexible decorative braid trim over the binding and hand-stitch in place, making a neat join somewhere close to a shoulder seam on the back of the shirt—not at center back where it will be obvious. You may stitch by hand or machine.

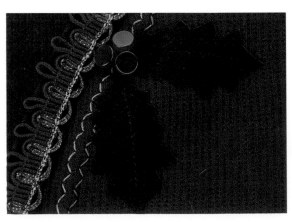

6. Cut and apply a 4-inch-wide strip of iron-on, tear-away stabilizer to the wrong side of each sleeve with the lower edges even.

7. Cut two 3½-inch-wide strips of pattern tracing paper, each 2 inches longer than the width across the lower edge of the sleeve. Center each strip over the zigzag stitching lines on page 151 and trace with a pencil, using as many repeats as necessary to fill the strip.

8. Position a strip on the right side of each sleeve and pin in place with the lower point of the lower zigzag line 2¾ inches from the lower raw edge of the sleeve (Figure 4).

Figure 4
Pin stitching pattern to sleeve.

9. Attach the topstitching needle and thread the machine with green topstitching thread. Stitch along the lower line on each sleeve. Change to gold topstitching thread to stitch the upper line. Carefully tear away the paper on the right side of the sleeve and lift and tear away the stabilizer on the underside. Use tweezers to remove any stubborn bits of paper or stabilizer.

10. Set the sleeves into the open armhole of the top and then stitch only one of the underarm and side seams in one long seam. Leave the other seam unstitched for now.

11. Measure the shirt lower edge and cut a 4-inch-wide strip of iron-on, tear-away stabilizer and a 3½-inch-wide strip of pattern tracing paper. Apply the stabilizer to the wrong side of the shirt with one edge along the lower edge of the shirt.

12. Trace the zigzag stitching lines onto the paper strip as directed for the sleeve. Position the paper on the right side of the shirt with the lower point of the lower zigzag line 2¾ inches above the bottom edge. Pin in place. Stitch as directed for the sleeves and remove the tissue and the stabilizer.

13. Complete the remaining underarm/side seam and press as needed.

14. Turn under and press 1¼-inch-wide hems on the sleeves and around the lower edge. Attach the blind-hem presser foot and sew the hem in place.

Appliqué & Embellishments

1. Remove the paper backing from the holly leaves. Position two at the center back and fuse in place. Stitch through the center of each one and sew three ¼-inch-wide buttons in place as shown in the photo.

2. Position the remaining leaves in pairs 4 inches below each shoulder seam in front and at the center of each sleeve just above the stitching. Fuse in place, topstitch through the center and sew the buttons in place.

3. Place the hemmed edge of the shirt around the ironing board and smooth out the shirt front. Remove the paper backing on the tree and center on the shirt front with the tip of the tree 1½ inches below the lower edge of the binding. Fuse in place.

4. Cut a 6-inch square of iron-on tear-away stabilizer and fuse in place on the wrong side underneath the tree.

5. Referring to the photo, cut and arrange 7–9 pieces of trim across the tree to imitate garland. Glue in place with permanent fabric adhesive and treat the cut ends with seam sealant to prevent fraying.

6. Adjust the machine for a narrow, medium-length blanket stitch or zigzag and sew around the outer edges of the tree, pivoting at the inner corners.

7. Sew the star button in place at the top of the tree and arrange the buttons as desired; sew in place.

8. Arrange sequins as desired and glue in place. Add a seed bead on top and sew or glue in place. Sew jingle bells to tree in desired locations. ✦

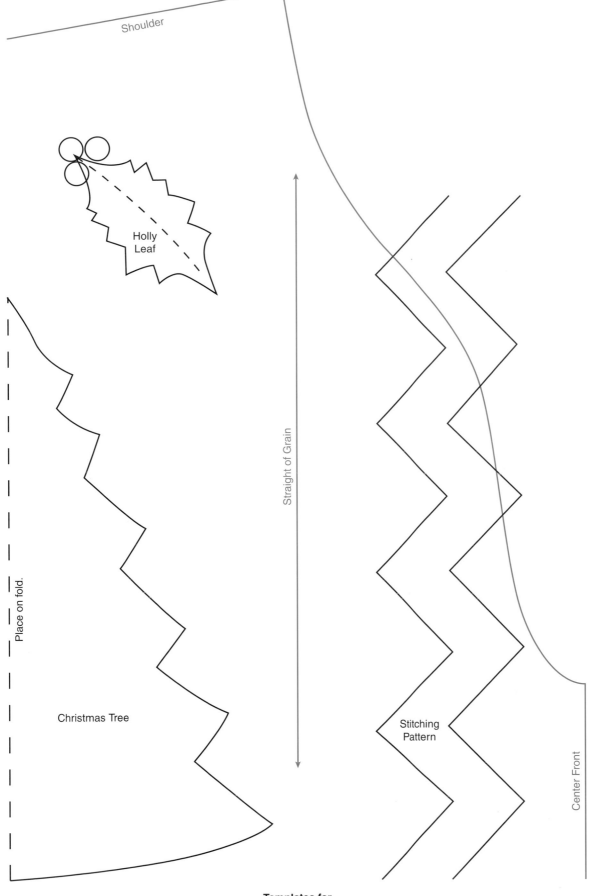

Shoulder

Holly Leaf

Straight of Grain

Place on fold.

Christmas Tree

Stitching Pattern

Center Front

**Templates for
Tree-Time Top**
Actual Size

Strippy Christmas Style

Design by Pauline Richards

Gather a few yards of red wool, a few Christmas fabrics cut into bias strips and some red and green buttons, and you will be set to create a timeless one-of-a-kind jacket for holiday affairs. Use a loose-fitting jacket pattern of your choice.

Finished Size
Your size

Materials
- Wear With All Jacket (www.saf-t-pockets.com) or your favorite loose-fitting shirt-jacket pattern with a collar in your size (with no center-back seam)
- Red wool gabardine or flannel in amount noted on pattern envelope
- Lining in amount noted on pattern envelope
- ¾ yard red-and-green woven plaid cotton
- ½ yard red-and-green cotton print
- ½ yard red cotton batik cotton print
- ½ yard green batik cotton print
- ½ yard green tone-on-tone cotton print
- Interfacing in amount noted on pattern envelope
- ¼-inch-wide paper-backed fusible web (Steam-A-Seam2 double-stick repositionable fusible tape recommended for ease of placement and application)
- Buttons for front closing as listed on pattern envelope
- All-purpose thread to match fabrics (two spools each of green and red)
- Bobbin thread
- Clo-Chalk
- Assorted red and green buttons for embellishment
- 2mm and 4mm twin needles, size 90/14
- Rotary cutter, mat and ruler
- Press cloth
- ¼-inch presser foot
- Basic sewing tools and equipment

Cutting

- Following the pattern guidesheet, cut the jacket from the red gabardine or flannel. Also cut the lining and interfacing pieces.
- From the plaid cotton, cut eight 1¼-inch-wide true-bias strips. Set the remaining fabric aside to cut additional strips if needed.
- From each of the cotton print fabrics, cut ½-inch-wide true-bias strips. Set remaining fabric aside.

Assembly

1. Apply interfacing to the jacket pieces as directed in the pattern guidesheet.

2. Turn the bias strips wrong side up and center a strip of ¼-inch-wide fusible web on each piece. Press lightly with an iron; cool and then remove the paper backing from each strip.

3. Referring to Figure 1, use the Clo-Chalk to mark 45-degree-angle guidelines every 3 inches on the upper jacket back and fronts.

Note: *These lines are not placement lines. In some cases a strip may be placed on or near a guideline, but not always.*

Figure 1
Draw guidelines on jacket pieces 3" apart.

4. Referring to Figure 2, position the bias strips wrong side down on the jacket fronts and backs, using the chalk lines as guides to keep the strips straight and positioning them the desired distance apart. *Make sure that the placement of the strips matches exactly at the center-front line on each front, not at the cut edge of the overlap.* As you place the strips, weave them so that some strips go over and others go under in a random fashion.

Figure 2
Use chalk lines as guidelines to position and keep strips straight and parallel on the jacket pieces.

5. When you are happy with the placement and all strips are straight and parallel to each other, fuse in place using a press cloth to protect the jacket fabric from overpressing or scorching.

6. Chalk-mark a stitching guideline through the center of each plaid strip on the jacket back and fronts.

7. Change to a 4mm twin needle and thread with two spools of red thread. Stitch through the center of all 1 inch wide plaid strips.

8. Change to a 2mm double needle and attach the ¼-inch presser foot. Using the foot edge as a guide, stitch through the center of all ½-inch-wide red strips

9. Thread the 2mm twin needle with two spools of green thread and stitch through the center of each green strip.

10. Replace the twin needle with a single needle and use the button-sewing feature (if available on your machine) to sew a button to each bias strip intersection. Match the thread to the color of button you are securing.

11. Refer to Figure 3 to reshape and narrow the collar pieces.

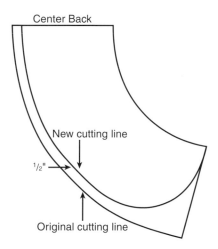

Figure 3
Reshape and narrow a pointed collar pattern.

12. Fold a remaining strip of plaid bias in half with wrong sides together and fusible web inside. Press to create a sharp crease (Figure 4).

Figure 4
Apply fusible web to center of
plaid strip. Fold in half and press.

13. Position the strip around the outer edge of one collar piece with raw edges even and pin in place. Stitch ¼ inch from the raw edges through all layers (Figure 5).

Figure 5
Sew folded bias to outer edge of collar.

Figure 6
Clip plaid strip to collar edge.

14. With right sides facing, sew the upper and undercollar together ⅜ inch from the outer raw edge. Turn the collar right side out. Beginning at the center back of the collar, clip the plaid strip to the collar edge, spacing clips ½ inch apart (Figure 6).

15. Complete the jacket following the pattern guidesheet directions. ✦

Wrapped in Ruffles

Designs by Karen Dillon

Layer strips of three elegant fabrics and add a row of elasticized stitching to ruffle them into an elegant shoulder wrap or scarf. You'll turn heads when you team it with a simple sheath or a formal gown for the Christmas or New Year's Eve ball. Add a matching bag for your evening essentials.

Finished Sizes
Wrap: One size fits all (approximately 8½ inches wide, 108 inches long, without elastic draw-up)
Bag: Approximately 4½ x 6 inches

Materials for Wrap & Bag
- 1½ yards metallic lamé
- ¾ yard coordinating-color 45-inch-wide cut velvet on a woven base cloth
- 3 yards 3-inch-wide lace or ⅓ yard all-over-patterned lace in contrasting or coordinating color
- 8 x 18-inch scrap cotton velvet or velveteen for bag
- 8 x 18-inch scrap lining fabric for bag
- 2¼ yards rattail cord for bag strap
- 1 (⅜-inch-diameter) velvet- or satin-covered button for bag closure
- 11-inch-long piece ⅜-inch-wide flat beaded trim for bag

- 1 spool elastic cord (not elastic thread)
- Woolly nylon serger thread in color to match lamé and 1 spool to match lace color
- 2 spools all-purpose serger thread to match velvet
- All-purpose thread to match lace color
- Perfect Sew liquid fabric stabilizer
- ¼-inch-wide paintbrush
- Waxed paper
- Liquid seam sealant
- Optional: electric blow dryer
- Water-soluble embroidery stabilizer
- Tailor's chalk
- Press cloth
- Rotary cutter, mat and ruler
- Serger with rolled-edge stitch (and differential feed if possible)
- Cording presser foot for sewing machine
- Basic sewing tools and equipment

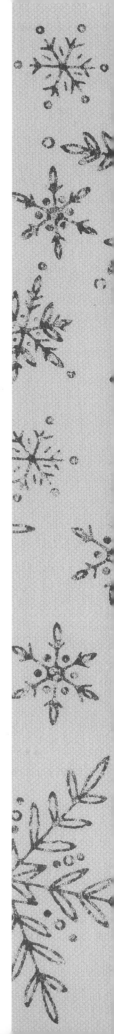

Cutting for Wrap & Bag

- From the lamé, cut enough 8¾-inch-wide strips to sew together for a strip measuring at least 110 inches long for the wrap. Cut one 3¼ x 10½-inch true-bias strip for the bag front and one 3¼ x 5-inch true-bias strip for the bag flap.
- If using lace fabric for the wrap instead of flat lace trim, cut enough 3-inch-wide strips to piece a strip that measures at least 110 inches long.
- From the cut velvet, tear three 5¼-inch-wide strips to sew together for a strip measuring at least 110 inches long. For the bag, tear one 2½-inch-wide strip across the fabric width. From the strip, cut one 2½ x 10-inch strip for the bag front and one 2½ x 5-inch strip for the bag flap.
- Cut the bag pieces from the velvet (Figure 1). Cut the same pieces from the lining.

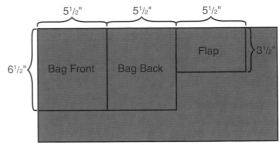

Figure 1
Cut bag pieces from velvet.

Wrap Assembly

1. Cut enough 2-inch-wide strips of waxed paper to go around the perimeter of the prepared strip. To prepare the lamé strips for serging, place the waxed-paper strips under the raw edges to protect the work surface. Use the paintbrush to paint a thin line of liquid fabric stabilizer along each raw edge of each strip. Allow to dry. Use an electric blow dryer to hasten the drying if desired.

Note: This step may not be necessary if you use a fabric other than lamé for the widest layer in the wrap. The stabilizer helps strengthen the lamé so that the rolled edge forms more easily at the serger

and prevents thread ends in the lamé from "poking out" at the finished rolled edge.

2. Adjust the serger for a narrow rolled-edge stitch and thread the upper looper with woolly nylon thread in a color that matches the lamé. Use matching serger thread in the needle and lower looper.

3. Use rolled-edge bias seams to sew the lamé bias strips together to make one long strip. Trim the strip to measure 110 inches. Cut the short ends of the strip so they are straight and perpendicular to the long edges (Figure 2).

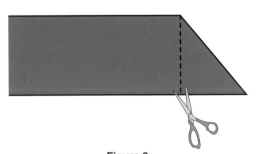

Figure 2
Trim angled ends of ruffle strip.

4. Repeat step 3 with the cut velvet strips (and with the lace strips if you cut strips from fabric rather than using flat lace trim).

5. Rethread the serger with thread that contrasts with the lamé; use woolly nylon in the upper looper and serger thread in the needle and lower looper. Roll-edge-finish one long edge. Begin by placing a small piece of water-soluble stabilizer under the edge so the stitching begins on the stabilizer and then catches the lamé. Serge for no more than an inch and then set the differential feed to 0.6 or the stretchiest position on your serger and continue stitching to roll the edge. When you reach a seam, reset the differential feed to neutral to cross the stitching line; then return the feed to 0.6.

6. Repeat step 5 with the remaining long edge of the lamé strip. Trim the strip to 108 inches and serge to roll the short ends as you did for the long edges. Apply seam sealant to the serger chains at each corner and allow to dry before trimming close to the fabric corners.

7. Trim the cut velvet strip to 108 inches and serge the short ends only, leaving the long edges raw. However, if you prefer, you can finish the long edges of the velvet with rolled edges, too.

8. Trim the lace strip to 108 inches; there is no need to finish any of the lace raw edges.

9. On each strip, measure and mark the center stitching line along the strip length on both sides of the lamé.

10. With all right sides facing up, center the lace on the velvet strip and then center these on the lamé. Pin the layers together with the pins across the stitching. Machine-stitch along the stitching line to secure the layers.

11. Cut a 56-inch-long piece of elastic cord and make an overhand knot at each end. On the wrong side of the stacked fabric strip, mark the center and quarter-points with a pin at each edge. Divide and mark the elastic cord at the center and quarter-points.

12. Adjust the sewing machine for a narrow zigzag stitch with a 2.5 stitch length. The width of the zigzag should be just wide enough to clear the elastic cord when you stitch over it. The stitches must not pierce the elastic. Attach the cording foot.

13. Insert the elastic cord through the center hole or groove in the cording foot. Holding onto the knot behind the presser foot, begin zigzagging over the cord and then pin the knot to the fabric end to hold it in place while you work. As you continue to zigzag over the cord, stretch the elastic cord so that the quarter-marks match as you go (Figure 3).

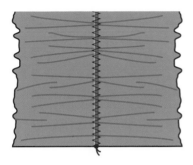

Figure 3
Zigzag over elastic cord on wrong side of layered fabric strips.

14. To secure the ends of the elastic, turn them back onto the fabric and stitch across the ends several times.

15. Place the wrap around your shoulders and use a pretty pin to secure it, or try wearing it as a scarf.

Bag Assembly

Note: Use ⅜-inch-wide seam allowances.

1. Adjust the serger for a narrow rolled-edge stitch and thread the upper looper with woolly nylon thread in a color that matches the lamé. Use matching serger thread in the needle and lower looper.

2. Roll-edge-finish each long edge of each strip of lamé. Begin by placing a small piece of water-soluble stabilizer under the edge so the stitching begins on the stabilizer and then catches the lamé. Serge for no more than an inch and then set the differential feed to 0.6 or the stretchiest position on your serger and continue stitching to roll the edge. Repeat with the remaining long edge of each strip.

3. Draw a line down the center on the wrong side of each of the two lamé strips with tailor's chalk. Center a velvet strip on the right side of each piece of lamé and pin in place. Adjust the machine for a basting-length stitch. With the wrong side facing up, stitch the layers together along the chalk line on each pair (Figure 4).

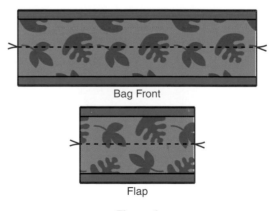

Bag Front

Flap

Figure 4
Baste velvet strips to lamé strips through center.

4. Draw up the bobbin thread on the larger piece so that the strip measures 6½ inches long through the center of the piece. Tie off the threads to secure. Gather the smaller strip to measure 3½ inches long and tie off.

5. On one of the 5½ x 6½-inch velvet pieces, use tailor's chalk to draw a centerline through the length of the piece. Center the lamé/velvet ruffle on top, pin in place and machine-stitch through all layers. Repeat with the shorter velvet piece and the short ruffle for the flap.

6. Center the beaded trim over the stitching line on each ruffle and hand-sew in place.

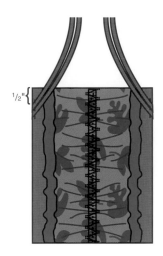

Figure 5
Baste cord ends to bag front.

7. Cut the rattail cord into two equal lengths. Arrange them side by side and tie two overhand knots with 6 inches between the knots (3 inches from the center of the cord).

8. Position the cord ends ½ inch below the upper short edge of the bag front and machine-baste in place (Figure 5).

9. With right sides facing, sew the ruffled velvet rectangle to the remaining velvet rectangle, rounding the corners as you stitch. Trim the seam to ¼ inch and zigzag the seam allowance layers together. Turn right side out. Press as needed, using a press cloth to protect the fabric nap.

10. Sew the bag lining rectangles together in the same way, but use a scant ½-inch-wide seam allowance so the lining will fit smoothly inside the finished bag. Do not turn the lining right side out. Turn under and press ⅜ inch at the upper edge of the lining.

11. Cut a 1-inch-long piece of elastic cord and form into a loop. Machine-baste loop at the center of one long edge on the right side of the flap rectangle. With right sides facing, sew the flap to the flap lining, rounding the corners as you stitch. Trim the seam to ¼ inch and zigzag the seam allowance layers together. Turn right side out and press from the lining side, taking care not to damage the velvet.

12. With right sides facing, pin and sew the flap to the upper edge of the bag back (Figure 6).

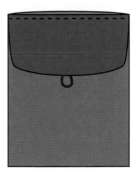

Figure 6
Stitch flap to upper edge of bag back.

13. Turn the flap up, turning the seam allowance into the velvet bag and continuing along the front upper edge. Baste the seam allowance in place.

14. Tuck the lining inside the bag with wrong sides facing and slipstitch the upper edges together

along the front edge and along the flap seam line on the bag back (Figure 7).

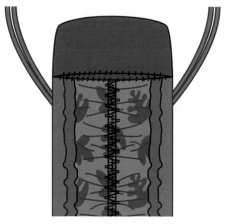

Figure 7
Slip lining inside bag and slipstitch upper edge to bag front and along flap stitching line.

15. Sew the button in place so the loop fits around it securely. ✦

Holiday Cardigans

Designs by Lyn Weglarz

Transform a sweatshirt into a cozy Christmas jacket with appliqué, embroidery and button embellishments. Tea-dye a white shirt to add visual interest and a homespun touch.

Finished Size
Your size

Materials
Note: *Purchase your sweatshirt in one size larger than normal, since removing the bands to turn the shirt into a cardigan causes some shrinkage in size. Also preshrink the sweatshirt before you begin.*

- Sweatshirt 1 size larger than normal (see Note above)
- ⅛ yard Christmas fabric for cuffs
- ½ yard total assorted Christmas fabric scraps for appliqués (large enough to accommodate appliqué shapes)
- ½ yard lightweight fusible web without a paper backing (see Notes at right)
- 3½ yards ⅝- or ⅞-inch-wide grosgrain ribbon
- All-purpose thread to match sweatshirt and ribbon
- Clear monofilament thread
- White paper
- Embroidery floss to coordinate with Christmas fabric or ribbon
- Embroidery needle
- Optional: buttons for embellishments
- ¼-inch-wide paper-backed fusible web
- Optional: hook and eye for neckline closure
- Rotary cutter, mat and ruler
- Basic sewing tools and equipment

Notes: *If you plan to dye a white shirt, read Dye It below before purchasing the shirt and dye. If fusible web without a paper backing is unavailable, substitute water-soluble embroidery stabilizer.*

Dye It
If you wish to tea-dye your sweatshirt for a mottled look, purchase a polyester/cotton blend, since the dyeing results will be more uneven, like the shirt shown. Use Dritz/Dylon Tea Dye or Dylon Cold Water Dye—Koala Brown. Follow the package directions to dye the shirt. Allow it to dry thoroughly after the final rinsing.

Cutting
- Cut away the ribbing at the neckline, lower edge and wrists of the sweatshirt.
- Mark the center front and cut along the line to turn the shirt into a cardigan jacket (Figure 1 on page 166).

Figure 1
Cut away ribbing. Cut through center front.

- Measure the lower cut edge of the sleeve and add 1 inch. Using this measurement, cut two 4-inch-wide strips from the Christmas fabric for the cuffs.
- Enlarge the heart and star templates on page 169 and trace onto white paper. Cut out. Use the pattern pieces to cut the desired appliqué shapes from the Christmas prints and from the fusible web. Examine the projects shown for shape selection and placement, or plan your own using the shapes provided.

Assembly

1. Turn under and press ½ inch at the front edges and around the neckline and lower edge of the cardigan.

2. Beginning at the inside right-front neckline edge, pin the grosgrain ribbon ¹⁄₁₆ inch from the fold. Fold a miter in the ribbon at each corner as you position and pin the ribbon all the way around the outer edge. Trim excess ribbon when you reach the beginning point, leaving enough to turn under for a neat finish. Stitch in place ⅜ inch from the turned edge of the cardigan (Figure 2).

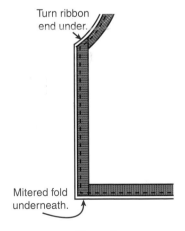

Turn ribbon end under.

Mitered fold underneath.

Figure 2
Cover turned edges with grain ribbon. Stitch ³⁄₈" from edges.

3. With 2 strands of contrasting-color embroidery floss, do a long (about ¼ inch) running stitch ⅝ inch from the turned-and-stitched, ribbon-faced edges.

4. Fold each cuff in half with right sides facing and short ends even. Stitch ½ inch from the raw edges and press the seam open. Turn under and press ⅜ inch along one edge of each cuff (Figure 3).

Figure 3
Turn under and press ⅜" at one edge.

5. With right sides facing and seams matching, pin the raw edge of a cuff to the cut edge of each sleeve. Stitch a scant ⅜ inch from the raw edges. Press the seam toward the cuff. Apply ¼-inch-wide fusible web to the turned edge of the cuff. Remove the paper backing, turn the cuff to the inside and fuse in place with the folded edge along the stitching line. Working from the right side, topstitch ¼ inch from the seam line through all layers.

6. With 2 strands of embroidery floss, do a long running stitch ¼ inch above the upper edge of each cuff.

7. With the fusible web (or water-soluble stabilizer) facing the right side of the fabric appliqué, pin and stitch the two together a scant ⅛ inch from the raw edges. Clip curves and points. Make a slit in the fusible web or stabilizer (Figure 4).

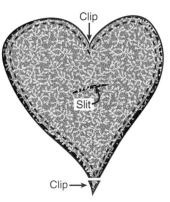

Figure 4
Sew fusible web to right side of appliqué.

8. Turn the appliqués right side out and finger-press the turned edges. If you used stabilizer instead of fusible web, trim away the center of the stabilizer, leaving about a ⅜-inch allowance all around. The remainder will wash out in the first laundering.

9. Arrange the appliqués as desired on the cardigan front and back, referring to the project photos for ideas. If you used fusible web, fuse the pieces in place following the manufacturer's directions. If you used stabilizer, pin the appliqués in place and thread the machine with clear monofilament thread in the needle. Adjust for a blind-hem stitch and sew the appliqués in place as shown in Figure 5.

Figure 5
Sew appliqués in place with
blind-hem stitch on machine.

10. Embellish the appliqués with running stitches as desired (see photos).

11. Add button embellishments as desired. ✦

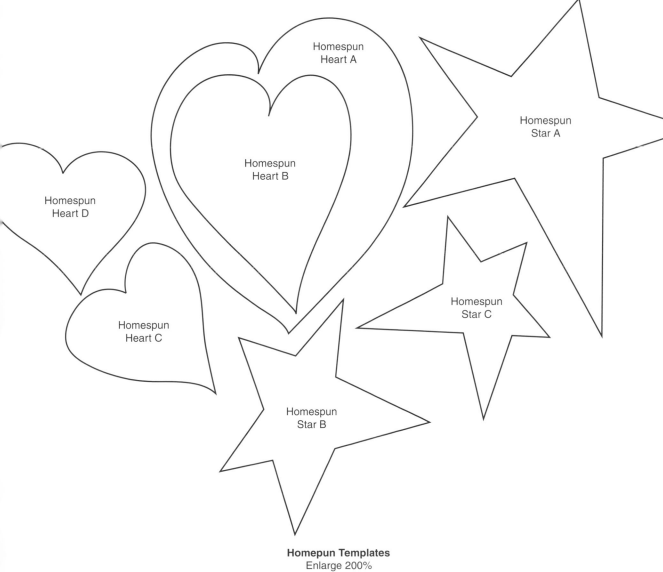

Homespun
Heart A

Homespun
Heart B

Homespun
Heart D

Homespun
Heart C

Homespun
Star A

Homespun
Star C

Homespun
Star B

Homepun Templates
Enlarge 200%

Pretty Packages

Design by Lorine Mason

Brightly wrapped packages dance across the back and front panels of this delightful child's sweatshirt. Ribbons and bows decorate the parcels holding tight the promise of wonderful surprises inside. Multicolored glass beads add a bit of sparkle.

Finished Size
To fit child

Materials
• Long-sleeved red sweatshirt for child
• ¾ yard Christmas print for packages
• Short lengths ⅛- and ¼-inch-wide satin ribbon in colors to coordinate with Christmas print
• Glass E beads in assorted colors
• All-purpose thread to match fabrics
• ¼-inch-wide fusible web tape
• 8-inch square paper-backed fusible web
• Water- or air-soluble marking pen
• Red embroidery floss
• Hand-sewing needle
• Permanent fabric adhesive
• Cutaway embroidery stabilizer
• Rotary cutter, mat and ruler
• Basic sewing tools and equipment

Cutting
• Fold the sweatshirt in half, right side out, and press along the center-front fold. Unfold the sweatshirt and cut open along the pressed line.
• Trim away the bottom ribbing from the sweatshirt.
• Round the lower center-front corners of the sweatshirt, using a small plate to mark the cutting lines (Figure 1). Cut each corner along the marked lines.

Figure 1
Cut sweatshirt at center front and use edge of
small plate for pattern to round the corners.

- From the Christmas print, cut an 8-inch square. Apply the 8-inch square of fusible web to the wrong side following the manufacturer's directions. From the prepared square, cut two 3-inch squares, two 2 x 3-inch rectangles and two 1½ x 2-inch rectangles for the packages.
- Measure the distance around the sweatshirt edges from right upper-front corner to left upper-front corner and multiply the measurement by 2 to determine the cut length for the ruffle. From the Christmas print, cut enough 3-inch-wide straight-grain strips to equal the measurement determined.
- Measure the circumference of the neckline, aligning the measuring tape with the bottom edge of the neckline ribbing. Add 36 inches to the measurement and cut enough 1½-inch-wide bias strips from Christmas print to equal the measurement. Sew the strips together with bias seams and press them open.

Assembly

1. Using ¼-inch-wide seam allowances, sew the ruffle strips together to make one long strip. Press the seams open.

2. At each short end of the strip, turn under and press ½ inch. Fold the strip in half lengthwise with wrong sides facing.

3. Machine-baste ¼ inch and ½ inch from the raw edges through both layers. Fold the ruffle in half crosswise and mark the center with a straight pin or the marking pen.

4. Beginning just below the neckline ribbing seam line, pin the ruffle strip to the right side of the sweatshirt. Match the center mark to the center back of the sweatshirt. Draw up the bobbin threads from each end of the ruffle to gather it to fit the front and lower edge. Adjust the gathers evenly and pin in place.

5. Stitch the gathered ruffle to the sweatshirt using a ⅝-inch-wide seam allowance (Figure 2).

Figure 2
Stitch ruffle to sweatshirt edges.

6. Press the seam allowance toward the sweatshirt all around.

7. Zigzag- or serge-finish the raw edges of the seam allowance together, including the raw edges of the ribbing at the center fronts, for a neat inside finish.

8. Use permanent fabric adhesive to glue the seam allowance to the inside of the sweatshirt, including the ribbing edge.

9. Fold the 1½-inch-wide bias strip for the neckline trim/tie in half lengthwise with wrong sides facing and press. Turn in ¼ inch at each long edge and stitch the layers together close to the folded edges on each side of the strip. Fold the strip in half crosswise and mark the center with the marking pen.

10. With the center mark matching the sweatshirt center back at the neckline, position and pin the strip to the sweatshirt. Align the upper edge of the strip with the lower edge of the neckline ribbing and leave the excess at each end for the tie. Stitch in place along both edges of the bias strip (Figure 3).

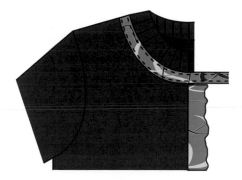

Figure 3
Sew binding to neckline below ribbing.

11. Trim both ends of the strip at a 45-degree angle.

12. Using a hand-sewing needle and an 18-inch-long piece of red embroidery floss, do a blanket stitch around the ribbing where it joins each sleeve and just above the bias trim at the neckline. With each stitch, pick up a glass E bead and slide it into place next to the fabric before taking the next stitch (Figure 4).

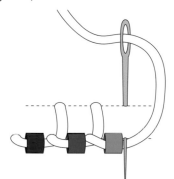

Figure 4
Beaded Blanket Stitch

Package Appliqués

1. Divide the squares and rectangles into two identical sets, one of each size in each set. For each package, cut a 3-inch-long piece of ¼-inch-wide satin ribbon and apply ¼-inch-wide fusible web to the back following the manufacturer's directions.

2. Remove the backing paper and center each ribbon on a square or rectangle. Fuse in place.

3. Referring to the photo, arrange one set of packages on the left front of the sweatshirt and fuse in place when you are pleased with the arrangement. Adjust the machine for a closely spaced medium-width satin stitch. Pin cutaway stabilizer to the wrong side of the sweatshirt under the packages. Satin-stitch over the package raw edges, pivoting carefully at the corners.

4. Make bows in the narrow ribbons and hand-sew in place at the top of each package.

5. Arrange and fuse the remaining three packages on the sweatshirt back; add bows. ◆

Fabric & Supplies

Page 86: *Angelina Poinsettias—* Beacon Adhesives Inc. Gem-Tac glue; Embellishment Village Angelina Fibers; Esterita Austin's Fusible Art Quilts Misty Fuse; Sulky of America Solvy water-soluble stabilizer and decorative threads

Page 98: *The Birds' Christmas—* Palmer/ Pletsch Perfect Fuse Sheer interfacing and Perfect Sew liquid embroidery stabilizer; OESD embroidery designs

Page 20: *Pinwheel Candies—* C&T Publishing fast2fuse lightweight nonwoven interfacing

Page 10: *Christmas Carryall—* The Warm Co. Steam-A-Seam2 paper-backed fusible web

Page 15: *Christmas Countdown—* Beacon Adhesives Fabri-Tac permanent fabric adhesive; Embroidery Central Cactus Punch Christmas Holidays 3 Advent Calendar embroidery designs; Prym Consumer USA Collins Wonder Tape basting tape and Dritz iron-on numbers; Sulky of America rayon embroidery thread and Fabri-Solvy Fabric-Like Water-Soluble Stabilizer; Velcro USA Inc. VELCRO brand Fabric Fusion hook-and-loop fasteners

Page 102: *Christmas Framed—* Embroidery Central Anita Goodesign Holly Wreath #Hdpcd13c and Holly Element #Hdpcd4; Fairfield Processing Corp. Soft Touch

pillow form; National Nonwovens WoolFelt; Sulky tear-away stabilizer and Sulky rayon embroidery thread; Therm O Web HeatnBond Lite iron-on adhesive

Page 66: *Christmas Sew-Phisticates—* Husqvarna Viking Designer 1 sewing machine; The Warm Co. Warm and Natural batting

Page 164: *Holiday Cardigans—* Blumenthal Lansing Co. Favorite Findings button embellishments; Esterita Austin's Fusible Art Quilts Misty Fuse

Page 58: *Homespun Christmas—* Fairfield Processing Corp. Soft Touch pillow form; The Warm Co. Warm and Natural batting and Lite Steam-A-Seam2

Page 26: *Jingle Bell Cards—* Foss Manufacturing Co. LLC Kunin Felt

Page 94: *Partridge on a Pillow—* Pellon Consumer Products Wonder-Under fusible web

Page 36: *Pet Hang-Ups—* Beacon Adhesives Fabri-Tac permanent fabric adhesives; Michael Miller Fabrics Inc. #C1551 Pink Michelle Meow, #C2635 Pink Paw Print Stripe, #C2636 Pink Heart Print and #C2612 Fuschia Distraction

Page 131: *Pieced Elegance—* Beacon Adhesives Fabri-Tac permanent fabric

adhesive; Exotic Silks/Thai Silks printed velvet #36LP/5075 and silk dupioni #6W/205; Prym Consumer USA Collins Wonder Tape basting tape; The Warm Co. Steam-A-Seam2 Lite fusible web tape

Page 6: *Poinsettia Warmers—* Beacon Adhesives Fabri-Tac permanent fabric adhesive

Page 170: *Pretty Packages—* Beacon Adhesives Fabri-Tac permanent fabric adhesive; The Warm Co. Steam-A-Seam2

Page 106: *Snowmen on Ice—* DMC quilting thread and needles; Pellon Stitch-n-Tear stabilizer and Wonder-Under fusible web

Page 30: *Sock-It-to-Me Knit Wits—* Fairfield Processing Corp. Poly-Fil Low-Loft batting

Page 152: *Strippy Christmas Style—* Saf-T-Pockets Wear With All Jacket pattern; The Warm Co. Steam-A-Seam2 fusible web tape

Page 78: *'Tis the Season—* Beacon Adhesives Fabri-Tac permanent fabric adhesive; Bonavista Fabrics Regal Stripe, Regal Checks, Regal Rounds and Regal Floral fabrics; Exotic Silks/Thai Silks silk dupioni #6W/205; Expo International tassel trim #IR2567BR; gimp #IR1901CB, twisted cord with lip #IR2548BR and tassels; Prym Consumer USA Covered Button forms

Sewing Sources

The following companies provided fabric and/or supplies for projects in this book. If you are unable to locate a product locally, contact the manufacturers listed below for the closest retail or mail-order source.

Adhesive Products Inc.
(510) 526-7616
www.crafterspick.com

Beacon Adhesives
(914) 699-3405
www.beaconcreates.com

Blumenthal Lansing Co.
(563) 538-4211
www.buttonsplus.com

Bonavista Fabrics
(323) 562-8500
www.bonavistafabrics.com

C&T Publishing
(800) 284-1114
www.ctpub.com

Clover Needlecraft
www.clover-usa.com

Criswell Embroidery & Design
www.k-lace.com

DMC
(973) 589-0606
www.dmc-usa.com

Embellishment Village
(877) 639-9820
www.embellishmentvillage.com

Embroidery Central
(800) 428-7606
www.embroidery.com

Esterita Austin's Fusible Art Quilts
www.esteritaaustin.com

Exotic Silks/Thai Silks
(800) 722-7455
www.thaisilks.com

Expo International
(800) 542-4367
www.expointl.com

Fairfield Processing
(800) 980-8000
www.poly-fil.com

Foss Manufacturing Co. (Kunin Felt)
(800) 292-7900
www.kuningroup.com

Husqvarna Viking
(800) 358-0001
www.husqvarnaviking.com/us/

Michael Miller Fabrics
(212) 704-0774
www.michaelmillerfabrics.com

National Nonwovens
(413) 527-3445
www.nationalnonwovens.com

Newark Dressmaker Supply
(800) 736-6783
www.newarkdress.com

Oklahoma Embroidery Supply & Design (OESD)
(888) 223-6943
www.embroideryonline.com

Palmer/Pletsch
(800) 728-3784
www.palmerpletsch.com

Pellon Consumer Products
(800) 223-5275
www.pellonideas.com

Plaid Enterprises
(800) 842-4197
www.plaidonline.com

Prym Consumer USA
www.prymdritz.com

Saf-T-Pockets
(503) 761-6460
www.saf-t-pockets.com

Sulky of America
(800) 874-4115
www.sulky.com

Therm O Web
(847) 520-5200
www.thermoweb.com

VELCRO USA Inc.
www.velcro.com

The Warm Co.
(425) 248-2424
www.warmcompany.com

Special Thanks

We would like to thank the talented sewing designers whose work is featured in this collection.

Marta Alto
The Birds' Christmas, 98
The Gifted Mantel, 74
Hanky-Panky Stockings, 46

Pam Archer
Pinwheel Candies, 20
Christmas Sew-Phisticates, 66

Janis Bullis
Crazy for Christmas, 118
Jingle Bell Cards, 26
On, Dancer!, 51
Partridge on a Pillow, 94
Star Bright Place Setting, 124

Karen Dillon
Oh, Tannenbaum!, 134
Tree-Time Top, 145
Wrapped in Ruffles, 157

Stephanie Corina Goddard
Holiday Reverses, 112

Linda Turner Griepentrog
Christmas Carryall, 10
Sock-It-to-Me Knit Wits, 30

Lorine Mason
Poinsettia Warmers, page 6
Pretty Packages, page 170

Pat Nelson
Winter in Bloom, page 140

Pauline Richards
Strippy Christmas Style, page 152

Judith Sandstrom
Snowmen on Ice, page 106

Lynn Weglarz
Angelina Poinsettias, page 86
Holiday Cardigans, page 164
Homespun Christmas, page 58

Angie Wilhite
Mitten Gift Bags, page 40

Carol Zentgraf
Christmas Countdown, page 15
Christmas Framed, page 102
Pet Hang-Ups, page 36
Pieced Elegance, page 131
'Tis the Season, page 78